HOW TO
SUCCEED

(AND FAIL)

AS A WRESTLING
PARENT

A Detailed Guide For Supporting
Your Wrestler's Journey

DONOVAN PANONE

TABLE OF CONTENTS

INTRODUCTION

I've seen the nervousness before the whistle blows, the emotional rollercoaster during close matches, the disappointment of losing, and the immense pride of big wins. I've seen parents who freak out and those who hide their faces. I've seen parents who feel helpless, with no idea what to say after a loss or how to motivate their wrestler to stick with the sport. And I've felt all of these feelings myself, both as a coach and as a parent.

During my 28 years as a wrestling coach, there have been parents who got it right, many who got it wrong, and others who got it way wrong. I often tell parents that my job is not only to coach their kids, but also to coach them.

Having said that, I am not going to tell you how to parent your child. Every kid is different and it's a hard job being a parent (I know—I have three kids myself). But I've seen a few things over the years that I feel are valuable to share. This book is written as a collection of the observations that I have made as a coach and the experiences I have gone through as a parent.

You will learn about the process it takes to succeed in wrestling and the role you should play in your wrestler's journey. You will hear directly from wrestlers about their unique path, what it took to jump levels, and their parents' involvement.

After reading this book, my goal is that you will be confident in any situation, reduce any nervousness or stress you may have about wrestling, and strengthen your relationship with

5

your wrestler. Just as I coach each of my wrestlers to be their best, I also want to enable you to be the best wrestling parent you can be.

For your wrestler, my aim is to provide you with a resource that will help them reach their potential as well as learn the valuable lessons wrestling teaches about life.

My hope for you both is that you will grow to love the sport and all that it has to offer.

My Background

I started coaching in 1994 when I was 20 years old. My first 21 years as a coach were spent volunteering with two USA Wrestling youth feeder programs and a high school program. Although volunteering was fulfilling, I knew I had more to give. I found myself constantly studying the sport, developing new drills and ways to teach that would improve my wrestlers' learning curve. I knew I wanted to coach for a living and had always dreamed of starting my own gym.

I finally decided to follow my passion and opened Level Up Wrestling Center in Marietta, Georgia, in June 2015. Since opening, I've been blessed with the opportunity to coach wrestlers of all skill levels. From beginners who struggle for years to developing state and national champions, including Super 32 champs, Fargo champs and winners of Flowrestling's Who's #1. My experience also enabled me to coach the Team Minion travel team (which won several national events) as well as multiple Team Georgia teams that have placed as high as fourth in the nation. Through this process, I've been around all types of parents and I have seen the patterns of the successful ones.

More importantly, I'm also the parent of a wrestler who started when he was four years old. I've seen all the highs and lows of the sport—not just through the eyes of a coach, but also as a father.

My son David wasn't naturally gifted early on and had to

work hard for his success. In his first three years of wrestling, he only won three matches and lost 59. He went on to lose 76 of his first 90 matches. Fast forward to today, he is a three-time high school state champion, placed in several national tournaments and was ranked nationally. So on the talent versus hard work discussion, I feel that I have an authoritative opinion on the subject. I'll go into more detail about his story and how he found success later in the book.

I've seen a lot in my years of coaching youth and high school wrestling. I've seen parents both nail it and fail miserably. My experience, spanning from beginners to national champions and every level in between, provides me with a unique perspective that I hope will benefit you in your efforts to support your wrestler.

Why Kids Should Wrestle

Wrestling can have a profound effect on your child's life. Not only is it fun to compete, learn, and try new moves, but there is also a special bond wrestlers develop with each other. And, as this is an individual contact sport, there are valuable benefits that are unique to wrestling:

1. Anyone can do it – You are grouped by age and weight, so it doesn't matter if you are small, short, tall, or big. Every size and shape has a style that can be successful.

2. Everyone gets to participate – Unlike team sports like football and lacrosse, there is no riding the bench. No politics or favorites. Every wrestler has a chance to participate and compete.

3. They learn valuable life lessons

• **Personal accountability** – When you win, it's because you did it. No one else gets the credit; no one else is to blame.

• **Bouncing back from adversity** – Losing in a team sport is disappointing, but the loss is different when it's only you on the mat. Wrestling teaches you how to lose gracefully and, more importantly, how to quickly put the loss behind you and move forward.

- **Persistence** – Wrestlers learn not to give up when things get hard. There are no timeouts in wrestling matches, so it puts them in a situation where they have to dig in and fight to reap the rewards. And since it can take time to learn, it also teaches them to persist in efforts to keep improving their skills in order to find success.

- **Performing under pressure** – As they gain experience, wrestlers can easily compete in 50 or more matches in a season. They have to mentally prepare for each match, learn how to stay calm under pressure, and deal with the feelings of anxiousness and nervousness over and over again. This process will help them perform under pressure in life too. A successful wrestler will know how to approach a speech, a big meeting, or an interview because they learned how to step up when it's time to perform.

4. Real confidence is built – Being praised is fine, but it only lasts for so long. When a wrestler masters a skill, like scoring with a move they've been practicing or winning a match over a tough opponent, it's because of the work you put in.

5. Incredible conditioning – Wrestling uses every part of your body and is one of the toughest sports to train and compete in. Kids build core strength and great cardio. They will be in shape.

6. Great for other sports – Many get into wrestling because they are football players or involved in other sports and they want to improve their skills. Wrestling improves body awareness, balance, coordination, and the ability to control someone else.

7. Energy outlet – Kids have a ton of energy and they need a way to channel it. Wrestling practices and matches are non-stop with no down time.

8. Competitiveness – If they are competitive by nature, they will love wrestling. Competing and winning against another individual is fun and brings a great sense of accomplishment.

9. Fun — It's fun to win, it's fun to compete, and it's fun to learn and execute new moves. While it's an individual sport, there's also a unique camaraderie that wrestlers have both with kids on their team but also those they compete with.

How to Read This Book

Whether you skip around between sections or read it cover to cover, I've designed it as a handy reference that will provide value years down the road. Some sections are more applicable for parents of younger kids, while other sections are more useful for parents of older wrestlers. I've written some sections for casual wrestling parents and others for those who are highly involved. Regardless of your child's level of participation, my hope is that you will find useful information and words of encouragement that will enhance your family's experience in the sport.

Within each section, I try to provide items you can take action on. I may also explain a topic and say, "Okay, so what does this mean for you as a parent?" In order to get the most out of the book, I recommend highlighting or taking notes on the actions YOU will take as a result of reading this book.

Section I
THE PROCESS
OF SUCCESS

When I say wrestling success is a process, I mean there are multiple, repeatable steps that can be performed and, when consistently applied over time, will result in progress. That progress is measured in both winning more matches and learning life lessons that are unique to this sport.

But unlike simply perfecting a swimming stroke, baseball swing, or throwing a ball, there are multiple factors involved. Not only is another wrestler trying to rip your head off while you are performing these skills, there are psychological dynamics of being the only person out there. There is nobody to pass the ball to and no timeouts to recover mentally. The whistle blows and it's on. This means the path toward success is much more complex than other sports.

Additionally, each wrestler has their own unique personality, body type, way of learning, and natural skills that all need to be taken into account. Not everyone will wrestle the exact same style or develop at the same rate. How far your wrestler chooses to take the sport is up to them. However, these are the core principles I have seen over the years that have proven results no matter what level they choose to strive for. It's this process that we will deep dive into now.

The First Step: Develop the Love

When you truly love doing something, you put your passion, heart, and soul into it. Wrestling is a tough sport. Very tough. To be successful, especially at the highest levels, you need to embrace the whole process. You need to love the grind: the wins, the losses, the hard work put into practice, the blood, sweat, and the tears.

Now, this doesn't mean you'll enjoy the losses or the grueling practices. Nobody likes to lose. Nobody likes to get beaten up at practice and then run sprints, or do extra conditioning when they're already exhausted. But you learn to appreciate what the hard work brings. You learn to love the grit of being in a tough match, fighting through positions, and staying calm through adverse situations. You learn to love the feeling of sweat pouring down your face. You may even get a little excited to wipe the blood away if you cut your forehead during a match. Wrestlers are a different breed.

This isn't to scare away a new parent to the sport. It's not like that in the beginning. But as you climb the levels and love the process of improving, you embrace all the little nuances of that grind to the top. There is a feeling of confidence you gain by doing the right things and by doing the hard things. That confidence is just a taste of the joy and exhilaration you feel when you win a big match or tournament. That feeling of having your hand raised makes it all worth it.

But in the beginning, it's much simpler than that. The joy and love of wrestling comes from different places for different kids. Some examples include:

• **A joy of the sport's physicality** – There is a raw human exhilaration derived from physically competing and controlling someone else. It's hard to describe and it's not for everyone; but for those who enjoy it, they really enjoy it.

- **Learning new moves and counter-moves** – The quest toward mastery is never-ending and the challenge of it is one reason that wrestling is fun. And, like in a chess match, there is an infinite series of moves and counter-moves that keeps the brain stimulated.

- **The chase up the ladder** – Like a good video game, there is something satisfying about mastering a level and unlocking a new one. The chase is almost as satisfying as the winning itself.

- **Confidence and pride** – These are gained from both success and overcoming challenges. Mastering a move, winning a big match, dominating your opponent, winning a medal at a tournament, and coming back from a loss are all great sources of satisfaction and growth.

- **A coach inspired them to be great** – I know this happened for me. It wasn't until I had a coach believe in me that things started to click.

- **Relationships** – There is a deep camaraderie that comes from working hard together and challenging each other as individual competitors that is different from team sports.

Helping your child develop a love for wrestling should be your No. 1 focus in the early years. As he or she gets older, your child's motivation will be rooted in the positive association with the sport that they developed when they first started.

Does "positive" mean that everything went their way? That they won all of their matches, never got hurt, they were praised for everything, and never told they did anything wrong? No. But parents often confuse having a positive experience with "happiness," so they shield their son or daughter from hard challenges that could lead them to being uncomfortable or unhappy. It's natural to want to protect your child from negative experiences, but this will hurt them in the long run. Dealing with adversity is the biggest life lesson that wrestling teaches.

Many parents think that if their child loses matches, it means they will have low self-confidence. Sure…if they lose all the time and never learn how to bounce back, it can lead to this. But by learning how to lose and how to win, they will start making progress. These incremental gains build confidence and will start to counteract the feeling of losing. So to have a positive experience with the sport, kids need to learn how to embrace losing as an opportunity to learn. Real confidence comes from accomplishing hard things, executing what they have learned, and the feeling of making progress.

My biggest advice to you in order to help them develop a love for wrestling is to not take it so seriously early on. Be involved by getting them to practice and attending their matches, but let them explore the sport on their own and just focus on having fun first. If they stick with it, at some point it will click and they will need to be the ones to make the choice to dedicate themselves to it.

Chapter 1. What is Success?

Winning, right? The goal of a match is to win so success means you win all the time... wrong. Winning is definitely more fun and the feeling of losing sucks, but that's not the ONLY way you measure success. If winning was the most important thing, then you would find the easiest tournaments and just stick with those. The process of learning how to improve, overcoming adversity, and climbing the ladder to higher levels is ultimately what wrestlers take away from the sport into life. These lessons are the ultimate definition of success.

But in order to climb that ladder, it means you have mastered a level by winning, then finding new challenges. Tougher matches, harder tournaments, and the climb continues until you are at the top. And the great thing about wrestling is that the top is always moving. You can reach the pinnacle of winning Olympic gold and there is going to be another wrestler training to knock you off.

Let's be honest, you are reading this book because you want to figure out the secret to success for your wrestler both in the short term and the long term. Both in how to win more matches and in learning the valuable lessons the sport provides, in order to become a better person and more successful adult.

I will give you all the secrets. But you have to do me a favor. When you read things you may not agree with, take a second and think about what I'm saying. Because some of what I tell you may be hard to hear.

Here it goes…the results of youth wrestling matches DO NOT MATTER. Yes, you can feel pride if your six-year-old wins state or even Tulsa Nationals, but in the long run those results don't mean anything. College coaches are not recruiting at youth events. At the time, it matters to them and the work they put in to try and win does matter. I'm not discounting that at all. But as you will read in this book, most kids are losing wrestlers in the beginning and many still go on to achieve high-level success when they are older. So if you are freaking out during your seven-year-old's match because they are diving for shots or won't get their head off the mat, just take a step back and relax. How they perform when they are young is not that big of a deal.

What does matter? The process. What is most important is that they learn **how** to succeed. That they learn how to handle wins and losses. Partially from an emotional standpoint, but more importantly from an action standpoint. If they learn these lessons now, they will develop a foundation for improving and thus win more matches in the long run. They will build confidence, not only in their wrestling abilities, but also in the work they put into any task. They will see the direct relationship between deliberate effort and winning, reinforcing the importance of hard work.

There are wrestling programs out there that show trick moves that work well at a young age. The thought is that if they win matches young, they will enjoy the sport more. But unfortunately that can create a false sense of security and build confidence in the wrong things. They will start only hitting that one move and once kids learn to stop it, their confidence will shatter. They build false expectations in themselves, and losing hurts even more when you think you are supposed to be good. You start losing to kids you've always beaten, because they learned how to defend that move and now you lack confidence. When the confidence you built is around your work ethic and your process for improving, you can always adapt and move forward. You can move up in competitive levels, knowing that you will figure out how to adapt and succeed quickly.

Ultimately, from the perspective of winning and losing, you want them to learn lessons at a young age that enable them to have success when they are in high school and beyond. Maybe they will wrestle in college, maybe they will not. Not every wrestler will go on to reach high-level success. I know parents and wrestlers who have done everything right, but the most the wrestler ever achieved was qualifying for state.

There are so many factors that go into it…natural physical talent, natural confidence, how much work they put in, emotional and mental skills, coaching situations, injuries, distractions, friends, financial resources, how much they love the sport, when they became serious about wrestling, and time. There is no perfect scenario. What I can tell you are the patterns I've seen and the ideal actions that take place. Some kids peak young and some find more of their success in college. Some will never reach their wrestling goals but will use those lessons to find immense success in life. As a parent, the important thing is to provide the best environment you can and let the process play out. Control what factors you can, but let the results happen and keep moving forward.

Focus on the Process, Not the Results

When kids and parents get so caught up in the result of a single match, or treat it like it's the most important thing in their life, I have to remind them that someone had to lose. Only two people wrestle in a match. Don't get me wrong, your wrestler should be giving everything they have to win the match. Winning is way more fun than losing, and learning how to fight for the win is very important. But it's also about having a healthy attitude toward losing and using it as a tool for learning. If you unnecessarily build up the importance of any particular match, all it really does is create undue pressure on everyone.

There are also several outside factors that can affect a match, including the ref making a questionable call, blood time allowing someone tired to catch their breath, the coin flip deciding who has the choice in the second period, landing in an awkward position and giving up points, etc. Most of these are not within your control. The reality is that you can wrestle someone 10 times and win nine of them, but that day happened to be the day you lost. That doesn't mean they are better than you or that all of a sudden you aren't good at wrestling. You just happened to lose that day. Win or lose, the wrestler should evaluate the match to figure out what they need to work on and keep finding ways to get better.

But aren't the results a measurement of making progress? Of course, but this sport takes time. Results do not happen overnight. Not only are they training their body and mind to perform a skill, they have to perform that skill when someone is trying to beat them up. And what if that opponent doesn't react the way they expect them to? Their body and mind has to process that and make a decision on the fly based on their experience. What if they haven't been in that situation before? They aren't trained for that yet. So now it's just about instinct. There is no time to stop and process thoughts in a wrestling match. You just have to wrestle. And while some kids are naturally strong, athletic and "scrappy," some are not. Most kids have to slowly grind at the sport to find success. All of these skills and training will take time to show the fruits of their labor.

It's funny. As a young coach and parent, I used to say, "They literally just worked that move in practice. Why aren't they hitting it during live wrestling?" Now that I'm more seasoned as a coach, I realize how long it really takes to execute a skill at a live pace. Drilling theoretically when the partner isn't fighting you is way different than doing it at high speed against someone who's also trying to impose their will on you. So all these skills, big and small, take time to develop. You can't look at each practice and think, "They just aren't getting any better." My advice is to **stay patient.** Look back on improvement in chunks of three to six months, not each practice or each match. Record their match videos and compare how they wrestle over time to see how their skills have evolved. What I like to do is ask a wrestler what the score would be if they wrestled themselves from a year ago. Usually it's a tech or a pin.

 Stay patient. Look back on improvement in chunks of three to six months, not each practice or each match.

Natural Talent and the Expectation Trap

You may have a wrestler who is naturally talented. A pure athlete who's gifted with natural strength or speed. These are great assets to have in any sport and, especially in wrestling, provide a strong base to build from. But winning early can also be a curse in the long run if the coach and parent is too focused on the results instead of the process. Sometimes a wrestler who wins early in their career doesn't have to work as hard as the others so they pull back on their effort. Often kids will do the minimum it takes to succeed. So the more they win, the more it reinforces the level of effort needed.

This a short-sighted view, though, because practices today are not to prepare you for the next tournament, but for the next years of your wrestling career. Eventually what often happens is that the kid who has been grinding for years will catch up to the kid with natural talent who developed a bad work ethic. Or puberty hits and the strength advantage they had no longer exists. Puberty is the great equalizer.

Whether your wrestler started off winning or found success after grinding for years, the expectations and pressure to win get elevated both from them and you. You go into tournaments expecting them to win and this can be a deadly trap.

Maybe they have been on a winning streak and a big tournament is coming up. They are excited and feel like they should win it. The first match starts and, boom, they get taken down right away. What happens? Instead of brushing it off, their world begins to crumble and they start to panic. The downward spiral of self-doubt begins.

"Maybe I'm not as good as I thought I was, maybe I actually suck at wrestling." As they panic, they aren't moving like they normally do and everyone starts yelling from the side of the mat. "My parents are yelling now so they must be mad at me; my coach is yelling 'Get up! What are you doing down there?' All this hard work…what was it for? I'm disappointing myself, I'm disappointing everyone. Oh crap, I was so worried about what everyone was thinking, I wasn't paying attention to the match. Now he's got a tight cradle on me. I can't get pinned. Everyone will be so mad at me. I'm trying to fight but it feels like I can't move." Pin!

Okay, maybe that's a little dramatic, but I've seen kids who are very good wrestlers melt down when expectations are too high and things aren't going their way. When you are used to winning all the time and then you start a losing streak, it can mess with your head. Self-doubt is hard to overcome unless you have a good coach or parent that can help you through it. Overly high expectations can lead to disappointment. Think about fans of football teams who have been so accustomed to winning. Every time they make a mistake or someone scores on them, or God forbid they lose a game, you would think the world is caving in. This is the expectation trap.

This doesn't happen to everyone, but hopefully you get my point. When too many expectations are in place and something goes wrong, it can devastate a wrestler and make it look like they are "not trying" or "giving up." So a few things can and should happen:

1. They learn how to deal with these subconscious emotions through experience. They will learn (either on their own or through the guidance of a good coach) how to wrestle through adversity and not feel sorry for themselves when something goes wrong. They also learn how to stay calm and just wrestle through a position instead of being overly focused on the "result" of being scored on.

They also need to learn how to tune out your voice when they wrestle and just focus on wrestling. They need to just accept each new situation as it comes and wrestle through it. "OK, I got scored on, no big deal. What's my job right now? Get hand control, escape and get those points back one at a time."

2. The parent shouldn't pile on more emotions in these situations. As a parent when your wrestler is new to the sport, you really don't have any expectations. You want them to enjoy it and stick with it. When they lose, you know it's because they are just new and don't know what to do yet.

But then something happens...they start winning. And winning is addicting. Not only do they get a rush, you do as well. So your competitive spirits are firing. But you should have a healthy outlook on being competitive. Don't get so fired up that those extra emotions turn negative and end up hurting your wrestler's chances to win.

3. The wrestler and the parent should let go of the concept of expectations. Winning in the past does not guarantee future victories. You have to go out and earn it every time. You should always expect a full effort, but treat each match as a new start. It's really just a shift of focus from expecting results (something not fully in your control), to the process of training, attempting the execution of skills, and learning from each match (things that are within your control).

And this cycle continues as you keep moving up the ranks—local, state, regional, national. Learning how to deal with these emotions are part of the process and the highest-level wrestlers still have these same emotions. Those that are the best at it learn to acknowledge how they are feeling and re-focus on being excited and grateful to have the opportunity to compete and showcase their talents.

 Winning in the past does not guarantee future victories. You have to go out and earn it every time.

The Progression of a Wrestler

Every wrestler starts with different tools to be successful. Some are naturally strong, some are fast, some are technical and some have great balance. And then some aren't blessed with the natural skills right off the bat. But they have the determination to get better and that's what will allow them to go further than someone with natural ability alone.

For some, it clicks right away. For the majority, however, it takes time to become good at wrestling. It is not an easy sport and it isn't for everyone. But, the lessons you learn and the feeling you get when your hard work enables you to win far outweighs the blood, sweat and tears it took to get there.

10 Steps Toward Wrestling Success

In order to enjoy the sport, a wrestler must find success. The practices are simply too hard and getting beaten every day isn't fun enough to treat it like a recreational sport. It's not that winning is the only thing, but pulling off moves and winning matches is a lot more fun than losing. Each wrestler will progress at different speeds, but what keeps them engaged is that they are making progress and can see themselves getting closer to their goals. To make progress, they should follow these steps.

Step 1: Show Interest – Some kids are attracted to wrestling because it's physical. Some enjoy the idea of learning "cool moves." Others like the aspect of individual competition. It could also be that their friends talked them into it. But at some level, there is a spark of motivation that starts it off.

Step 2: Learn the Basics – The basics are everything in wrestling. It doesn't matter how many moves you know if you can't master the basics.

Step 3: Get Beaten and Learn To Lose – Many first-year wrestlers only win a few matches and some do not win any. And while some seem to pick things up quickly, they still get their butts kicked by the kids who already have experience. Brand-new, youth wrestlers can and should go to beginner tournaments at first if available, but if they find early success, they should move on. The mind and body will adapt and settle on what it takes to achieve success. No matter how quickly a wrestler picks up the sport, you cannot be successful in wrestling without getting beaten and pushing through adversity.

Step 4: Get Beaten Some More – Whether in matches or with more experienced wrestlers in practice, you are going to take some lumps early on. For some, this may take a year or two before realizing what it takes to succeed.

Step 5: Decide You Want to Get Better – At some point a wrestler will make a choice. He or she either doesn't like the sport enough to push through the adversity or they decide they want to get better. Maybe in the course of getting your butt kicked, you pull off a move in practice or you get close to scoring, and that taste of victory was enough to motivate you to want it more. But at some point, the wrestler has to decide they want to improve.

Step 6: Work Your Tail Off – Now that the decision has been made, the next step is to put in the time and effort to get better. But you cannot improve at wrestling by just showing up to practice. You must be motivated to learn. And while practice is important, it's what you do outside of the room that will separate you from your competitors.

Step 7: Get Mat Time – This is one of the most overlooked, yet most important, ways to improve. There is a direct correlation to the number of matches you wrestle and your ability to succeed. You can't get better at wrestling by just showing up to practices.

Step 8: Breakthrough Moment – At some point there is an aha moment and something clicks to unlock the next level. This could be improving a certain technique, winning a big match, or simply overcoming a mental obstacle. Things become clear as you are winning more and gaining more confidence.

Step 9: Seek out Tougher Competition – You cannot move levels without this. I repeat. You cannot move levels without finding ways to get outside of your comfort zone and adapt to a new level of wrestling.

Step 10: Continuously Repeat Steps 4-9 – At each level you move to, you will face new adversity and will need to continue to push yourself in order to get better.

Nine Levels of Wrestling Success

So what does it mean to go to the "next level"? As you repeat the cycle of improving, getting beaten and improving some more; a youth wrestler will move up through different tiers of success. Eventually a wrestler will move on to high school and the cycle continues. How quickly a wrestler moves through these steps depends on the work put in, mat time, and the desire to progress.

Level 1 – This sport is fun, but I'm losing a lot.

Level 2 – I'm starting to win matches at beginner tournaments, but I'm getting crushed at open ones. It's hard, but I think I'm starting to get it.

Level 3 – I'm winning one to two matches each open tournament.

Level 4 – I consistently win two to three matches and I've placed in a couple of tournaments.

Level 5 – I am a pretty consistent placer with a couple of tournament wins under my belt.

Level 6 – I expect to win most local tournaments and matches.

Level 7 – State winner or placer; I am now traveling to seek out tougher competition and I win a few matches when I go. (Note: The attempt at Level 7 can help speed along the progress at Level 6)

Level 8 – I am starting to place in national tournaments and I dominate local ones.

Level 9 – I'm officially a national stud, placing and competing for the win every time.

Chapter 2. What is the Process?

So if we focus on the process and not the results, what exactly is this process? It is an intentional, repeatable cycle of steps that enable the wrestler to keep improving. Can you enjoy the sport at a basic level without being this serious? Sure. I know several wrestlers that started as kids and wrestled through high school without attempting to progress in the sport. They did the minimum and survived. But as their natural abilities ran out, their progress either flatlined or went backwards. They were passed by others who were working harder and the sport became less fun and less fulfilling.

These wrestlers usually look back on their careers either with regret that they didn't try hard enough or that "I just wasn't that good." If your wrestler takes this path, there is nothing wrong with it. Everyone makes their own choices. But if they want the sport to be more rewarding and are willing to put the time in, they can learn how to be great at something and achieve big goals.

A basic framework of the process of success is listed on the next page.

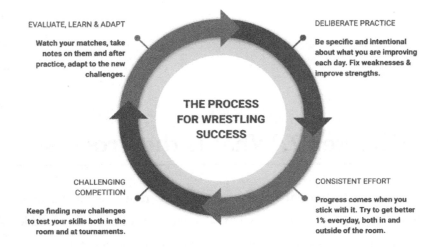

EVALUATE, LEARN & ADAPT

Watch your matches, take notes on them and after practice, adapt to the new challenges.

DELIBERATE PRACTICE

Be specific and intentional about what you are improving each day. Fix weaknesses & improve strengths.

THE PROCESS FOR WRESTLING SUCCESS

CHALLENGING COMPETITION

Keep finding new challenges to test your skills both in the room and at tournaments.

CONSISTENT EFFORT

Progress comes when you stick with it. Try to get better 1% everyday, both in and outside of the room.

In addition to this cycle of steps, the following factors are infused throughout the process. They are the difference between being good and becoming great.

- Taking ownership
- Sacrifice
- Balance
- Expanding the comfort zone
- Keeping it fun
- Having gratitude

Deliberate Practice

Deliberate…intentional…purposeful. These are all words used interchangeably that basically mean to improve at something specific every day. The key is not just going through the motions, but picking one to two small things to improve on. You would be surprised how much of an impact this has. There is a huge difference between just showing up to practice and placing direct attention on improving something specific.

In order to grow and improve at any skill, it has been proven that you need hours and hours of deliberate, purposeful practice. How many hours? In Malcolm Gladwell's book *Outliers*, he coined the "10,000 hour rule." According to this rule, it takes 10,000 hours of practice to become a master in any particular field. But is this actually true?

This rule was derived from a study by Anders Erickson performed in 1993 of Berlin violin students. Erickson went on to write a book called *Peak: Secrets from the New Science of Expertise*. In his book, Erickson debunks this "rule" and says that it was taken out of context. 10,000 was simply the average amount of hours that the best violinists had spent on solitary practice by the time they were 20 years old. In his book, he explains that what truly made people masters and sped up the learning curve was the amount of deliberate practice they put in. For some to achieve mastery it took much less than 10,000.

Erickson goes on to explain that "deliberate practices that are designed to achieve a certain goal consist of individualized training activities—usually done alone—that are devised specifically to improve particular aspects of performance." **An hour of performing or basic practice "is not the same as an hour of focused, goal-driven practice that is designed to address certain weaknesses and make certain improvements."** So it's not about the amount of hours, but what you put into those hours.

So what does this mean as a parent of a wrestler? While some coaches have started utilizing these principles, not all have. Many simply go through the motions each day of warming up, drilling, live wrestling and conditioning. You should definitely not interfere and tell the coach how to run their practice. But you can ask your wrestler questions and help them learn how to be deliberate on their own. You can encourage them to evaluate how they are doing and what areas need to be worked on.

Depending on their age, this may not be realistic. A seven-year-old is rarely going to be able to construct a set of skill-based goals and create a daily action plan. But that doesn't mean you can't be curious and ask them questions. I certainly wouldn't smother them with these. But you can still sometimes ask "What did you guys work on in practice tonight? Did you understand it? What do you think you need to work on?" This could lead to you encouraging them to ask the coach for help after practice. Even if it isn't fully systematic, they learn to ask for help and take action to improve.

It really depends on the personality of the child, but I've found that the ages between eight and 11 are when you will have the most impact as a parent in shaping their behaviors and habits. They are old enough to process things on an intellectual level, but aren't fighting for their independence yet.

Here are a few actions you can take as a parent to help create habits of being deliberate:

- **Have them get in the habit of taking notes after practice and matches.** If they have a phone, they can jot a few notes down in the Notes app or I like an app called Evernote. Even young kids without a phone can simply tell you to write down a few things or use a small notebook.

- **Encourage them to watch videos of past matches**. They can also take notes and ask their coach for advice.

- **Encourage goal setting and action plans.** Help them identify personal strengths and weaknesses to work on, or new skills that fit their style

- **Set goals for each practice.** Help them think about one or two things they want to accomplish in practice that day.

- **Get them to evaluate their wrestling.** Instead of telling them all the things you think they are doing wrong, ask them questions that help them to start owning the process. You can ask what they think they need to work on, or about a situation that happened in a match. Or simply encourage them to ask their coach what they think they should focus on.

- **Compete.** Make sure they are attending the right amount

28

of competitions so they have an opportunity to evaluate their wrestling and learn. They should learn from mistakes, but also identify positives so they feel good about their wrestling, reinforcing behaviors they should continue.

- **Stay after practice to work on one thing for five to 10 minutes.** They can ask the coach for help or grab another wrestler to work on something (especially a position they may have felt during that practice). Ten minutes per day, multiplied by five days per week over a 16-week season, equals 800 minutes or over 13 hours of extra practice.
- **Private lessons.** These can be with one of your coaches or an outside training center. Not everyone can afford it, but it certainly can make a difference in how quickly someone makes progress.

Consistent Effort

I have wrestlers who come to the gym for a week and then you don't see them for three months, then they pop in again. These kids will never make real gains. The ones who see the most progress are those who are there consistently each week. So when they are young, parents taking them to practice is a huge part of the formula of success. Of course, if they haven't decided to be full-time wrestlers, this concept of consistent effort may only apply to the wrestling season. But it does apply to any sport or activity to which they have dedicated themselves if they want to be good.

The goal is to get 1% better everyday. This doesn't mean that the wrestler needs to practice every day. But it does mean that they are doing something to improve. Is it possible to find success without being all-consumed every day? Moderate success, sure. An athlete with some natural talent can simply practice with their team, do the minimum, and still win matches. They can even have a winning record. If that is all they want, then there is nothing wrong with that. But if they want to go beyond being "just a kid on the team" and find success at the higher levels to maximize their individual potential, then they will need to do more. It takes a different level of self-discipline to become elite. This could be as simple as good form on their push ups to getting extra reps after practice or doing all the little things right. One of the coaches at Level Up has a great quote: "If you want to be an elite wrestler, you have to do things elite wrestlers do."

When you are passionate and love the sport, doing little things daily comes naturally. You don't have to necessarily plan or schedule it. But it is more effective to be deliberate about it. Here are a few daily efforts wrestlers should be doing to maximize their success. They don't all need to be performed each day, but at least some combination of these should be done consistently. As mentioned several times, these need to be choices and actions they decide to do, but as a parent you can support these.

- **Mindset** – Daily journaling, goal setting, creating action plans, visualization, and practicing positive self-talk
- **Recovery/Mobility** – Ice baths after tough practices to reduce inflammation, using a Theragun or some other massage tool, stretching, or yoga.
- **Nutrition** – Healthy and balanced meals (proteins, veggies, fruits, daily supplements), healthy snacks, pre- and post-workout nutrition
- **Hydration** – Water, water, electrolytes, and water. Not only is this important for an athlete to replenish fluids from sweating, it maximizes recovery, overall energy and brain function.
- **Sleep** – One of the most important elements for an athlete. Getting seven to eight hours of sleep each night is critical for recovery after tough practices, but also provides you the energy to work hard the next day.
- **Video review** – Either reviewing their own match videos

or watching matches and clips on Flowrestling or YouTube.

- **At-home technical work** – Some wrestlers have a mat in their house where they work on skills either on their own or with a partner or sibling. Whether or not you should be directing these at home "practices" is very dependent on your child.

When they are younger, this may be totally fine and can be very helpful if they are receptive to it and buy in to the importance of extra work. Some kids will dutifully follow instructions and some will push back but eventually appreciate the extra work their parents had them put in. Others will also rebel completely and forcing them constantly will make them hate wrestling. You will just have to make a judgment call on how hard to push this.

- **Strength or agility training** – I recommend that wrestlers balance their training with some sort of strength training. This can simply be daily pull-ups and push-ups at home, joining a gym or getting a personal trainer.
- **Cardio** – There is some debate amongst coaches if longer distance running helps wrestling. Some feel wrestling is the best way to train for wrestling and some believe in running. Talk to your coach and draw your own conclusions.

Seeking Challenging Competition

Competing is a critical step in the developmental process. That's what wrestling is all about. This is not a sport like Taekwondo where progress is based on the teacher deciding you have done enough to earn the next level. If you never learn how to compete, you will be left behind developmentally and then practices become miserable if you are losing all the time. But at the same time, it's easy to get so caught up in it, compete too often and lose sight of the ultimate goal, which is to develop as a wrestler. You want to find a good balance between training, developing skills and competing.

In fact, I did a study for Team Georgia. There was a large

proportion of wrestlers who had USA Wrestling memberships, but were not competing at events. Or they had competed in novice events, but were not returning to move up into the open events. The primary reason parents gave was that they didn't feel their wrestler was ready and didn't want to hurt their confidence. Some coaches were buying into this also or were afraid to encourage their wrestlers to compete.

The study I did was to identify the relationship between participation and retention. Since the reasoning was that it was better to wait a season to learn the sport and "be ready" before competing, I wanted to see if those kids ever returned to the sport the next year. I had access to all the membership data and cross-referenced their USA Wrestling numbers with registrations for all the tournaments during the season. This included both beginner tournaments and open events. I then looked at how many of those memberships were renewed the following year. The data I found was overwhelming:

Of all first year wrestlers…

97% returned the next season when they attended at least one event.
Only 6% returned the next season when they DID NOT attend an event.

Of course some of the kids who didn't compete and didn't return probably didn't like the sport enough to attend a competition in the first place. But maybe if they had at least tried, they would be part of that 97% who returned the next year.

I'm not saying wrestlers should jump in the deep end right away. They can build up how often they compete and the skill level of their competition over time. But after they've learned the basics, they should start wrestling other beginners and learn how to compete.

The decision to begin competing in wrestling tournaments is somewhat child- and age-dependent. You want their first experience to be positive, but you also shouldn't protect them from doing hard things. Ultimately if they are truly going to enjoy the sport and reap its benefits, they need to be competing. Wrestling is a tough sport and kids need to feel like they are making progress in order to enjoy it. I've learned that making incremental progress is what motivates kids to stick with the sport. It isn't just about winning. It is about seeing their hard work pay off and knowing that, if they keep working, they will find higher levels of success. It's this chase for success that is more addicting than the winning itself.

On the flip side, if you don't feel like you are making progress, you can only take getting beaten up in practice so much until you decide it's not the sport for you. If a wrestler only practices, the kids they were even with at the beginning of the season will develop at a faster rate, and they will wonder why they aren't as good anymore.

To illustrate this point, take two kids at equal age, size, strength, athleticism, and skill levels who both practice all season. One competes at tournaments and the other only practices. By the end of the season, the one who competed will start beating the other one. The one who competed learned what it took to win. The one who competed felt the pain of losing and the thrill of victory so their practices were fueled by the hunger to both avoid the pain and capture that feeling of winning. It's then only natural that the one who competed is going to practice harder and more deliberately, with their reaction time and feel for positions also improving in this environment.

They also learn the valuable lessons of staying calm under pressure and adapting to adversity in the moment. The mental game is a huge part of all sports, but especially wrestling. Live matches are the only way they will learn these skills.

In addition to seeking out tough competition at tournaments, they should also find tough partners in practice in order to adapt to their surroundings. Wrestlers should always have three types

of practice partners:
1. People they can beat
2. People they are even with
3. People who can beat them

It can be tough at first to purposely find kids that will beat you in practice. Most kids will avoid this. A good coach will make sure they are mixing it up with different skill levels at practice and moving them with people who are one or two levels above where they are. But if the coach isn't doing this, as a parent, you should encourage your wrestler to do it for themselves.

Over the years, I've seen parents on the extreme ends of the spectrum. Parents hold them back from competing until they are "ready" or their wrestler finds early success and immediately starts touring them across the country. Both approaches are wrong.

Go compete, take some lumps, adapt, find some success, build confidence and then jump a level. Losing too much too quickly makes them think they aren't good enough for the sport. If it's too easy, it gives them a false sense of confidence and their skills won't improve. Too many losses in a row will mess with even the most naturally confident kid, so you need to find the balance. Feed the hunger and challenge them, but know when to pull back.

There is no perfect formula for the amount of losses they should take. I've heard some people say they want their kid to lose 50% of their matches so they stay challenged. I get what they are saying but it's kinda dumb. Kids can get "used to" losing all the time and not figuring out how to win. Ideally, you want them to learn how to fight and win and adapt to their surroundings before moving them up to the next challenge. Adapting doesn't necessarily involve winning every match. It just means understanding how to win, while also learning from losses and setbacks, is a critical part of the process.

Competition Tips

In order to learn how to compete, and foster that healthy appetite for competition even at a young age, here are a few pointers.

- **When to start competing** – Ideally they should have a move they know in all positions, including a basic takedown, takedown defense, how to score on top and how to get out from bottom. From my experience in most seasons as a volunteer coach, this took about a month. Learn the basics and go try out your skills against other beginners. They don't need to learn a lot of moves first. They also don't need to be so good that their chance of winning is 90% or better. They just need to feel somewhat comfortable and get out there and scrap. You shouldn't force them if they aren't ready but, at the same time, you should show them it's not scary. It's also important to make sure they know that tournaments are for practice. They aren't that big of a deal if you don't make them a big deal. If needed, have them watch a tournament before competing so they can see their friends wrestle and have fun.

- **Beginner/Novice Tournaments** – Depending on what state you reside, they may be able to compete in beginner tournaments. These are usually for first- and second-year wrestlers and it allows them to get matches with those equal to them in age, weight and experience. Once they start winning or placing high in two or three of these, they need to start mixing in the open tournaments. They will only be as good as the competition around them. In Georgia, one problem has been parents holding their kids back from moving into the open tournaments because they are afraid they will get discouraged and quit wrestling. Wrestling only beginners will give them a false sense of security and they will be afraid to wrestle the "tough kids." Once their years of experience force them to the open events, losing will make them want to quit because they didn't learn the value of losing and facing challenges.

- **Number of youth/middle school matches per season and year** – How many matches should they get in a season? This also depends on the wrestler, but "mat time" is an important element to getting better. I had a seventh-grade wrestler a few years ago who had four years of experience. He kept getting so mad when he lost matches. He was infuriated, frustrated, and just didn't understand why after four years he was still losing so much.

I asked him "How many months out of the year do you wrestle? He said, "I play football also, so about three." I said, "Okay and how many matches do you think you've wrestled each season?" He thought for a little and didn't know so I said "You have been at practices, but most seasons you have only been coming to like three to four tournaments. So if you are going 0-2 or at best 2-2 you are maybe getting like 10 matches in a season. So in four years, you've maybe had 40 total matches. That is not a lot of experience. My son (whom he looked up to) gets 75+ matches in a single folkstyle season and then wrestles year-round. You only wrestle during the season so you are kinda restarting the learning process each year. You are not allowed to be this frustrated when you have barely wrestled any matches in your career."

He got what I was saying and developed a more patient mindset. From there his wrestling improved and he made an effort to wrestle more matches as well as started wrestling freestyle in the spring. After that he found a ton more success and wrestling was more fun.

So what is the right amount of matches in a season? It's going to depend on the wrestler. Parents are always worried about "burnout" but that isn't necessarily a result of too many matches. Sure, there is a point of diminishing returns and a limit to what is healthy mentally and physically. But burnout is the result of many factors, which I cover later in the next section, "The Journey."

In the first couple of seasons I would shoot for at least 20 to 30 matches annually. Many youth tournaments have round-robin brackets where there are four to six kids and you wrestle all of them, where some are double elimination brackets. So if you are averaging four matches per tournament, that's five to seven events each season. From their third to fifth season of wrestling, 30 to 60 matches in a season is good or 50 to 75 in a calendar year. At this point they will be winning more so will naturally have more matches.

As they improve you can certainly up that number. If they are making progress or feeling confident after a winning streak, you should capitalize on the momentum. Some kids are hungrier than others and you can also enter two weight classes for extra mat time or they may end up on a travel dual team where they are guaranteed six to eight matches. But also make sure you are asking them what they want to do. Some weekends they may need a recharge and some weekends they will want to do more. There is no exact magic number and if they start going year-round, there will always be opportunities to wrestle.

If they wrestle in the spring freestyle/Greco-Roman season, they will see more mat time. You just have to play it by ear and make sure they are getting quality matches. In my experience, I would say a good maximum for kids ages 10 to 14 years old is 50 to 75 matches in a folkstyle season or 75 to 100 matches in a year. You want to leave time between events to evaluate, learn, and train specific areas to improve on.

- **High school wrestling** – Once they enter high school their season will be dictated by the coach and whether or not they are on the varsity team. If they decide to become a year-round wrestler or wrestle freestyle/Greco-Roman in the spring and summer, they will naturally pick up more matches. There are usually several events in the preseason, spring and summer. I would check with your club coach to determine what events make sense for your wrestler. If they are still a newer wrestler, the volume of mat time may be important. For a more experienced wrestler, quality may be more important than quantity.

Evaluate, Learn, and Adapt

Adapting to tough competition in the practice room and in matches is critical to making progress and jumping levels in wrestling. When you evaluate your performance against them and train to beat them, your sights are set higher and the level of your training will rise. If you train to beat kids at a lower or similar skill level, that is the level you will stay. Compete at a level, train and adapt to it, then jump to the next.

But there is a process to it, whether it's conscious or subconscious. Part of learning to improve is developing a consistent habit of deliberate and honest evaluation of yourself, win or lose. This can take time and it also takes maturity. If you ask an eight-year-old what went well in their matches and what can be worked on, the response will likely be, "Uhhh.... hmmmm...I don't know."

At a young age, it's hard for kids to be systematic about this whole thing. They just know wrestling is fun. So keep it fun for them while also teaching them about the process of improvement. Remind them that losing and making mistakes are just part of the process of learning. It can be hard to watch as a parent, but I'll say it again—someone has to win the match and someone has to lose. To say someone has "experience" means it's happened over time and through both wins and losses, successful decisions and mistakes. You should not expect perfection out of your wrestler and they should not expect perfection out of themselves either. This doesn't mean they have to enjoy losing. It's more about learning how to reframe the reaction to it.

Instead of getting mad, they should realize that you can't go back in time to wrestle the match again, so they instead should figure out what needs to be worked on in practice to improve for the next time. Here are some basic tips for consistent improvement.

- **Ask Questions** – As a parent, ask them questions about the match. It's easier to tell them all the things you saw that they need to work on, but avoid that temptation. It's important that they start thinking about ways they can improve for themselves. Simply ask, "What do you think you need to work on?" It should also be "What did you do well?" Evaluating yourself should include both areas to work on as well as positives that should be replicated in the future. Successes should be recognized.

- **Taking Notes** – As they get a little older, they can start being more formal about the process. They may not want to do it at first, but this is where your role of helping them stay accountable can come in. Wrestlers should keep a wrestling notebook or use an app on their phone to save notes. There can be match notes, practice and camp notes, goals and action plans and even a daily wrestling journal. Simply transitioning the thought from their brain into words helps them recall what they need to work on and starts the process of taking action.

- **Video Review** – This is another major habit they should get into and a part you can play. This can be done immediately after their match but also at home afterwards. Keep in mind that some kids are uncomfortable watching themselves while others are eager to watch. Part of this has to do with age and maturity. You should record their matches either way and when they are ready, they can start watching back. I recommend that they still jot down a few notes and they can also ask their coach for feedback on specific positions.

- **Modeling Others** – As part of the evaluation process, I recommend to my wrestlers that they find a high-level wrestler to look up to who has a similar style or a style they like. They should watch their matches and highlights to learn how to emulate how they wrestle. Take notes and then work on specific things at practice that you saw that wrestler do. I also recommend taking younger wrestlers to go watch local high school or college matches. This will not only expose them to better wrestling, but also give them older kids to look up to.

Major Factors That Influence the Process

There are several factors that influence success. Self-discipline, motivation, work ethic, and mindset are all very important. But this is a book for you, the parent, and the best way for you to be part of the process:

Taking Ownership

This is arguably the most powerful of all factors that influence success. Once the wrestler decides for themselves that they want it and they start taking action on their own, they make massive gains. Unfortunately, it's also the most mysterious of all the factors. You can't really make them take ownership, otherwise they are still doing it because you said so. It's hard to pinpoint why it fully clicks. It could be that a coach inspired them, their friends influenced them, or they just got sick of losing. Sometimes it comes from attending a big event like the state tournament or a national event. But the most important thing is that they are the ones who are driving the ship, not you.

How can you foster the concept of taking ownership?

- **Involve them in decision making** – Even if you already know the answer, make them feel like they have a say. This could be the decision to attend a certain tournament, go to a camp, start strength training, or even deciding what type of healthy foods to buy.
- **Help them set their own goals and create an action plan** – When they are young, this can be really basic. But when they set the goals, you can now say "Are you good with me helping you stay accountable to reach these?"

40

- **Have them determine their weekly training schedule, including both practices and extra work** – Post it on the refrigerator calendar or a shared online calendar.

- **Avoid being overly critical of their wrestling** – If you are having a conversation about their wrestling, avoid telling them what they need to work on. Instead, ask them what positions they think need work or what actions they are taking this week to improve.

- **Allow them to fail** – As parents, watching your child struggle or get upset is hard. We want them to succeed and it's a source of pride for us, so we often give them the answers or put them in positions to avoid failing. But if we are there to constantly protect them from failure or are the ones pushing them without their buy-in, they will never learn on their own. Learning through their own experiences creates a long-lasting association with the consequences of action or inaction.

More importantly, they are the ones in charge of figuring out a solution. They learn important problem-solving skills instead of having a parent tell them where they messed up and what they should do to fix it. You have more life experience than them. You will likely have an answer. But you don't need to be at the front of the class raising your hand vigorously for the teacher to see you. Hold the answer back sometimes and help them figure things out. You can be part of the conversion and help them think through it, but they need to be the ones to own solving the problem if you want them to learn how to succeed in wrestling and life.

If we are there to constantly protect them from failure or are the ones pushing them without their buy-in, they will never learn on their own.

- **Don't do everything for them** – When you feel the urge to do something for them because "It's just easier if I do it myself," you probably need to have them do it. These little

41

tasks and processes of taking ownership add up and build their confidence.

What if they don't want to go to practice one night? That's different. If they said they have a goal and they said they were committing to practice three to four days a week, then you are helping them stay accountable. If their action plan said they need to get stronger and are committing to 50 pull-ups a day, and they agreed you would help make sure they did it, that is your role to help them.

Ultimately, though, it's on them. If they fail to do the things they said they would do, then they will suffer the consequences. And when they don't achieve their goals, they will learn. You can be there to help them make that connection (without the "I told you so" tone). The best way I've found as a coach is to simply say "What do you think you can do differently next time?" This puts the ownership on them and also focuses them on a future goal, not beating them up about the past.

Having said all of that, while it's critically important for them to own the process, the highest-achieving wrestlers tend to have parents who are still involved in finding resources, training opportunities or events to wrestle in. They still are an active part of the process, just without the helicoptering and smothering. The wrestler should want to keep pushing themselves and there is a mutual collaboration with their parents. None of what the parent does really matters unless the wrestler wants it for themselves. Eventually if the wrestler goes on to wrestle in college, they will be on their own. They need to have established intrinsic motivation and independence before they leave if they want to be successful, both in wrestling and in life.

Sacrifice

If your wrestler is just getting started, then they haven't sacrificed anything yet. They haven't been "bitten by the bug" as one of my coaches used to say. They need to have fun first, enjoy the exhilaration of competing and develop a love for the sport. Once they have shown signs of saying "Okay, I want to be really good at this and do what it takes," this is when you can feed their hunger and get them to engage more.

At some point, there is going to be a conflict between what they need to do and what they want to do. A friend wants them to come over and play Xbox, but they have practice that night; or maybe there's a camp you signed up for and they are tired and don't want to go. This is a great opportunity for you to teach them the lessons of accountability and sacrificing in the short term for a long-term goal. This is one of the major roles of a wrestling parent. As I've mentioned, you should mostly be hands-off and let this be their sport and process. That said, holding them accountable to something they said they wanted is important.

As they move through the ranks and keep improving, the sacrifice is not only on them but will often be on you. Traveling to out-of-town tournaments, paying for extra training, sitting in a gym all day to watch them wrestle—these are all necessary if you plan to support their dreams. And you can choose not to do these things for sure. They can simply go to their local club practice a couple days a week and only attend the tournaments that are close to your house. If you do not support their desire to keep challenging themselves, though, it's very hard to achieve higher-level success.

Balance and the Quest For Greatness

It is easy to put blinders on as a parent and pour everything into supporting your wrestler's path to success. You can get caught up in competitiveness and doing everything you can to help them win. And that isn't bad. But sacrifice also comes at a cost.

One cost is time. Time spent on wrestling is also time not spent on other life skills, like having a job, learning about responsibility and money, etc. Weekends are spent at wrestling tournaments, not doing projects around the house, and learning how to pitch in or perform small do-it-yourself projects, etc. And this doesn't mean those skills won't be picked up along the way, but eventually the wrestling will go away and they need to develop other life skills and experience other things that may influence their path and career in life.

This doesn't mean not to sacrifice. If they take wrestling to a very high level, they will need to sacrifice things that other kids or teenagers do. And that can be healthy and teach the valuable lesson of working hard towards a goal. However, be careful and recognize when the sacrifice for greatness becomes an unhealthy obsession. Make sure to take the time as a parent to also teach balance and involve them in other skills or hobbies.

Expanding the Comfort Zone

Along the way, there will be periods that feel uncomfortable. Learning new things takes effort and is uncomfortable, hard practices are uncomfortable, taking risks is uncomfortable. They will need to get comfortable being uncomfortable as they grow and expand. They need to learn how to operate right outside of their comfort zone until they adapt and become comfortable again and then keep expanding.

As they get more serious about wrestling, they have to be vulnerable enough to seek out challenging partners in practice. They have to deliberately find ways to push their limits, go into "deep waters" and hit an emotional breaking point. This is the moment when their mind is telling them to stop and they continue to tap into those emotional reserves. It's when they push past this breaking point that they often find a whole new level in their wrestling.

As a parent there is not much you can do to affect this. Just be supportive if they come home upset after a tough practice or if they start getting frustrated. Remind them that it takes these moments to grow and achieve their goals and that you are proud of the hard work they are putting in.

Keep it Fun

It's easy to take wrestling too seriously. Winning requires hard work, discipline and sacrifice. But ultimately it's still just a sport. As my friend Phil Arnold, father of Gabe Arnold, always puts the following on his Instagram posts: #itsjustwrestling. I have had wrestlers in the past take it too seriously and it ultimately hurt their development. They were so focused on doing things "right" or "wrong" that they couldn't let themselves be fluid and feel things while they wrestled. They almost worked too hard. Sometimes you have to let go a little and remember that wrestling should be fun. If it ultimately isn't fun and fulfilling, why do it?

Of course fun doesn't mean that it's easy or just playing games at practice. And I also don't mean that every aspect is fun. Hard practices, cutting weight, and losing matches are definitely not fun. But you develop an appreciation for the process. You find fun in knowing you are improving, scrapping live at practice, play wrestling, getting into challenging scrambles, and mastering a new skill. In matches you find fun in scoring points and executing skills you've been working on.

A big part of the experience is also having fun with friends at tournaments and dual meets, both at the event but also traveling together and creating bonds that last a lifetime. I've heard several wrestlers tell me that they don't remember going to a specific tournament, but they do remember the car ride there joking around with their friends.

Of course as I've mentioned several times, winning is way more fun than losing. The thrill of victory is what fuels the competitive desire. You train and work hard because you want to win. But there is an interesting paradox with sports. When you focus too much on winning, it becomes less fun. You have to find fun in more than just winning. I recently heard a former

Olympic wrestler coach one of his kids after a tough loss and he said, "You have to want to wrestle more than you want to win." I thought that was great. The wrestler was so focused on winning that he choked at the end and got out of position. But when you let go and just love the art of wrestling, winning small positions and scoring points, the results take care of themselves.

From the parent's perspective, the biggest thing is for you to just remember to also keep it fun. Don't get so worked up yourself. Enjoy that you get to watch your child do something they love to do and have fun doing. Your attitude will rub off on them.

Having Gratitude

Penn State University is credited for starting the movement of the "attitude of gratitude," empowering success in wrestling. And it's rightly so. Their coach, Cael Sanderson, was the only undefeated wrestler in college (159-0) and went on to be an Olympic champion. Sanderson was hired in 2009 and as of writing this book, Penn State has won nine of the last 11 NCAA team titles and had 32 individual national champions. So naturally people wanted to understand their secrets and emulate that success. Every time a Penn State wrestler is interviewed after a big win, one of the consistent things they say is "I'm just grateful that I have the opportunity to compete and showcase my skills. Not everyone has this opportunity and I'm thankful for it."

The Harvard Medical School defines gratitude as "a thankful appreciation for what an individual receives, whether tangible or intangible. With gratitude, people acknowledge the goodness in their lives. As a result, gratitude also helps people connect to something larger than themselves as individuals—whether to other people, nature, or a higher power."

So what does gratitude have to do with wrestling?

Former Penn State wrestler Pat Higgins had the following to

say about his experience.

An attitude of gratitude was perhaps the most impactful lesson I learned. Applying gratitude daily is something that wasn't always easy for me at first. But, once I started practicing an attitude of gratitude, much of my life changed. I was able to start finding the good in everything, counting my blessings every day and among other things always felt I was improving. Even my worst practices were productive because I was grateful for everything. Wins were opportunities to be proud of my hard work, losses turned into lessons to make me better. Coach Cael used to have us write down something we were grateful for each and every day, and also encouraged us to write down two things specific to wrestling that we were grateful for. Maybe we hit a takedown we've been working on, or maybe we got close to a takedown on someone better than us. Whatever it may be, we should be grateful for it.

One thing I want to say about gratitude from my own experience is to let you know that gratitude means being grateful for everything, GOOD and BAD. It's even more important to be grateful for the bad things in life because those are what make us stronger, better or remind us of how great we have it. The pure ability to be happy means that we must also sometimes be sad. You'll never know happiness without sadness because they are two sides of the same coin. If you never lose a match, you'll never understand the happiness that comes from victory.

Now, that's not to say it will be easy to be grateful for everything bad. Some things are simply too difficult to bear at times. However, this is when gratitude for those around us becomes crucial—being grateful for the support we have, the people who love us, your faith, they become crucial aspects of an attitude of gratitude.

Sanderson, the decorated coach, expanded on how this mindset has been so impactful for his program and his wrestlers.

So, what does gratitude mean? I've thought a lot about it, for years and years. It just means that you think less about yourself. If I'm grateful, I'm going to think less about myself and more about others, and the opportunities I have…When you can take a step back and look at life like that, it can change your perspective. It takes the pressure off. You're just trying to get the most out of yourself and the most out of the blessings that you have.

Thoughts are tough. It's a battle. It's like a wrestling match in your head. But you can win those matches. Ultimately, we get to pick our attitude, we get to pick our perspective. We want to help our wrestlers to understand that, that it's their choice. When we go into a big match or go into a practice, they get to choose the attitude they bring. There's great power in realizing that's the truth. It's hard to accept it, too. Because now there are not any excuses. It's me. What I did, what I decided. We have a lot more power and control over our lives than we think. It's consistency and making good decisions. It's the small steps, where maybe we don't see the consequences or the benefits over a short amount of time. Those little steps come from gratitude. In the long run, those things are the difference-makers — over months, a year, a lifetime. It's those little things. And it all starts with our attitude.

This attitude also allows us to reframe how we think about matches. Instead of being nervous or worried, you become excited to compete. You have the opportunity to execute new skills or showcase your God-given talents and the training and hard work you've put in. This goes along with detaching from the pressure of results and allows you to wrestle with freedom.

Instead of being mad when you lose or get scored on, your attitude is to be grateful that you had that learning experience. Because without that experience, it wouldn't have revealed the positions you need to work on.

As a parent, you can also take this approach by reframing your reactions to experiences both negative and positive. Your child will model your behavior, especially at a young age. Help your child understand how to reflect or even write down what they are grateful for. Recognizing and appreciating what they have and the experiences they've gone through is a powerful lesson that not only will affect their wrestling, but their life.

Section II
THE JOURNEY

Now that you've learned what success requires, I want to give you some insight into what goes on in the mind of the wrestler. Because it's an intense one-on-one sport, wrestling can bring both exhilarating highs and devastating lows. How you handle these can affect their wrestling, as well as impact your relationship. In order to help you along the way, I've provided my insights from years of coaching, as well as excerpts from interviews with wrestlers who have found success and have gone on to wrestle in college. You will see that each wrestler's path is unique.

Additionally, there will be ups and downs that you will go through as you experience this sport as a parent. I will do my best to prepare you for this so you understand some of the emotions you will feel by sharing insights as well as my own personal story as a wrestling parent.

Understanding Your Wrestler

One thing I've learned from coaching all these years is that each kid is different. Sure, there are patterns and common personality traits, but they all have their own unique path. Some are naturally competitive, hate losing and find a way to fight; and some assume they are bad because they get scored on and feel helpless. Some are naturally confident and some have self-doubt. Some are detailed and perfectionists, and some are sloppy and undisciplined. Some learn fast and others take months or years to pick things up. Some work hard and some not so much. Some respond well to tough love and some tuck their tail. Some will cry when they lose, some will get pissed and some will show no emotion. Some need more structure, some need more autonomy. None of these are wrong. You just have to learn the language each kid speaks to find what makes them tick and will motivate them.

As they get older, they will start to mature physically and mentally. Embrace who they are. I recently had a parent tell me that a few years back, he was getting frustrated because his son didn't move or react fast enough when wrestling. This infuriated him for years because, in his mind, his son wasn't wrestling hard enough. I told him, "You know he's really just not a natural athlete and when you embrace this, you can help him develop a style that works." I hadn't spoken to him about this for a few years and he said this piece of advice was the best thing that happened to his son's wrestling and their relationship. His son's body matured and he ended up at 195 pounds. In turn, as a father, he was able to let go of false expectations of what he thought his son should be doing. His son developed a style that fit his body type and personality and ended up placing fourth in the state during his junior year.

They Are Not You—This is *Their* Journey

Parents tend to compare their kids to themselves. There is a bias that because you are a certain way (i.e. fast, strong, hard worker, visual learner, etc.) that your child will have the same tendencies. But they aren't you. They have a blend between mom and dad, as well as a product of their environment and experiences. Additionally, parents often project who they are now and assume their kid should already know certain things. But they forget who they were as a child and that they had to go through some tough situations first before becoming who they are today. So when your child screws up, there tends to be a sense of disgust or "I can't believe they did this." But when you were a kid, you did the same thing and made the same mistakes. This doesn't mean to not have high standards, but it does mean to have patience.

And if you have never wrestled, you won't understand the complex emotions that go on in their head. Wrestling is not like other sports. There is great glory that comes with winning and accomplishing something hard, but it can also be devastating when you lose. Practice can also be grueling. Not just the physical hard work (which is very hard), but the frustration of not getting the moves down right away and the constant emotional rollercoaster of winning and losing during live wrestling. Not only does it hurt to lose in general, it's also in front of your friends and family.

So my point of all that is…

• Expect that there will be ups and downs on their journey. Don't expect it to be perfect.

• Expect that they will probably lose in the beginning. Some will lose more than others. Be ready to encourage them to stick with it and keep plugging away. Don't avoid matches just because they lost in the past. Stay the course.

• Stay patient knowing that kids learn and mature at different rates and all have unique strengths & weaknesses.

• Have empathy knowing that this is a tough sport, unlike any other. But at the same time don't coddle these emotions. Help them learn how to mature through these experiences to keep improving and become stronger as a result.

• Push them when they need to be pushed and back off when it's time to back off.

• Have an open line of communication so your wrestler is not afraid to talk to you. The parent and child need to be in sync.

• Always remember that it's their journey and not yours.

Chapter 3. Perspectives From the Wrestler's Journey

In addition to my perspective as a coach, I felt it would be valuable to hear from the wrestlers themselves. I've talked to a few who recently graduated high school or have finished a couple years in college. These wrestlers started either as young kids or in middle school and have since found success at a national level. They all started with different levels of natural talent and had very different paths. Most were losing wrestlers when they first started.

For each wrestler, I have included a small part of their journey so far and the answers I felt would provide you the most value.

RJ Weston

Age Started: 4-5

Youth Accomplishments: One-time state champion.

High School Accomplishments: Two-time state champion (injured one year). Cadet National champion and most outstanding wrestler in Greco-Roman, third in freestyle; Junior national third place in Greco.

College: Redshirt freshman at University of Northern Iowa (Div. I).

Did you have success when you started? When did you start to excel and what caused that?

I started around four to five years old. When I was four, it was

53

mostly just rolling around at practice a couple days a week. At five I started doing tournaments. I was always generally decent, but struggled when moving up to the next age group. As I got older, I had a good record but always choked in big matches. I didn't place in state until seventh grade (about 13 years old). This corresponded with the decision I made to wrestle year-round. I used to only wrestle during the season and played other sports, but I decided I wanted to dedicate time and effort into wrestling. This is something I decided for myself. It didn't come from my parents.

Around this time, because I decided I wanted to be really good and was sick of not performing well at big events, I also started doing mental imagery. I would take the time to picture myself in tough situations where eyes were on me and there was pressure. I got mental reps picturing myself winning instead of wrestling not to lose. I'm still working on this today.

Tell me about ups, downs and emotions you felt along the way, as well as actions you took.

When I was about seven years old, I remember wrestling the first four tournaments going 0-2 each one, so my record on Trackwrestling was 0-8. I had already wrestled in tournaments for two years so this really hurt. I remember telling my dad that "I don't want to sit on the sidelines at state this year." So before every tournament on Friday, I would go into the wrestling room and would hit 100 singles on the right side, 100 on the left, then 100 double legs. I still didn't place at a single tournament, but I did start winning more matches. I made a little progress and started going 1-2 or 2-2. The only tournament I placed in that year was the state qualifier, but this was a big deal for me to qualify for state. I had reached a goal I wanted that season. I realized at a young age that it's all on me and my effort. So I started setting new goals and moved up little by little. I also started competing in two weight classes at tournaments for mat time.

RJ Weston "Looking back, the biggest thing that kept me motivated was new goals. When I accomplished it, my attitude was 'What's next? Back to work.'"

Right before seventh grade started, I went year-round and started training at Level Up. I showed potential and knew I needed to challenge myself, so I wrestled at Super 32 (one of the toughest national events there is). I went 0-2. But I felt what a national event was like and knew what I needed to work on. A couple of months later, I won a smaller national event called Dixie Nationals. When state came around that year, I had a really tough, national-level wrestler in my weight class. I could have dodged him and moved weight classes, but I decided to go after him. I got close, but ended up losing 2-1. This just fueled my training. In eighth grade, I was one match from placing at Super 32, won state for the first time, and ended up winning 14U nationals in Greco-Roman. I was third in freestyle and was very close to making a USA Pan-Am team.

But wrestling can be tough. As soon as you feel like you are on top, the bubble bursts and you are back to the drawing board. I had a goal of being a four-time high school state champ, but I lost in the semifinals my freshman year. But after it was over, I was back to setting new goals. Looking back, the biggest thing that kept me motivated was new goals. When I accomplished it, my attitude was "What's next? Back to work."

My next goal was winning Fargo. I worked hard and had to deal with a giant roller coaster of emotions. There were always battles of self-doubt and being emotionally broken in the practice room, but I always battled back. The summer of my top-end Cadet year (16U), I was on the Team Georgia dual team for Cadet National Duals. I didn't have the best event. I didn't wrestle great, lost a few matches, and ended up getting hurt. My entire body was cramping up for hours and ended up at the emergency room. Fargo was only a month away. After a week off, I recovered and only had three weeks to make adjustments. I was really focused on trying to win a Greco title. I could have had self-doubt from the duals, but I just focused on improving little things and I knew those past losses didn't mean I was destined to lose again. The freestyle tournament came first and after picking up a couple wins I was in the zone. I ended up taking third place. I built off that confidence and won the Greco title, not being scored on the entire tournament and won the Most Outstanding Wrestler award. **Sometimes after big adversity, you end up wrestling your best.**

What role did your parents play in your wrestling? What did they do that helped or hurt your success/progress?

Growing up, my dad was a volunteer coach so naturally he coached me. He loved me and always wanted the best, but finding the divide between the roles of parent and coach was hard. My dad didn't know how to do that and it hurt sometimes. In fourth or fifth grade, he would yell at me during and after matches and he couldn't control his emotions. He may not have been yelling volume wise, but it sounded like yelling to me. My mom said he wasn't allowed to coach me during matches anymore. She wanted him to just be my dad. So he got an assistant coach to help in the corner. Sometimes, I would run off the mat upset after a loss and my dad would try to run after me, but my mom held him back so I had time to cool off. But it was hard for him to keep quiet. He would sit on the opposite side of the mat from the coach and still yelled stuff. So I finally got the courage up to tell him that his yelling was distracting.

The year I was wrestling to make a Pan-Am team at 14U nationals, my dad really got in my head. I won Greco, but in the finals of freestyle I was getting headlocked. My dad was on the opposite side of the mat and even though he wasn't yelling, he kept shaking head. I really wanted my dad to be proud of me, and him shaking his head showed he was disappointed. I remember looking at him and was focused on this instead of wrestling. I ended up getting teched. In the true second match, it happened again. I was so focused on my dad being disappointed when he would shake his head. After this tournament, we talked about it and he realized how much the emotions he was showing during my match was affecting my wrestling. He started stepping back and just being a supporter and it made a big difference, both in my wrestling and our relationship.

The feeling of disappointing my dad is something I don't want to feel again. And while it did motivate me in the room to work harder sometimes, it also would demotivate me and was a big distraction. I was already naturally motivated though. If I didn't love wrestling I would probably have just stopped. Luckily my dad never forced me to go to wrestling practice. I always wanted to be there. So really most of these issues were about matches. Even at home, my dad would bring things up that happened during matches and I would get mad at him. I started resenting him and didn't want to talk to him. Every time we talked it was about wrestling and it started affecting our relationship. At one point we finally talked about separating the roles and he did better at it. He learned that his emotions were just making everything worse and he learned to back off and it improved my wrestling in matches. I really believe you need to have a relationship with your parents where you can have open and honest communication about how you are feeling and what you need to be your best.

Jake Piccirilli

Age Started: 9

Youth Accomplishments: None. Placed fourth twice at kids state tournament.

High School Accomplishments: Three-time state placer (sixth, fourth and third). Never placed in a national tournament.

College: NCAA Div. II National qualifier as a true freshman (21-10 record beating three ranked opponents). Jake is currently a sophomore and ranked No. 9 in the nation.

Did you have success when you started? When did you start to excel and what caused that?

I was horrible when I first started and got my butt whooped a lot. I was so frustrated with getting whooped that I was thinking about quitting and got pushed to the point of it not being fun. I had to develop a mindset to where I knew I was getting better. Sooner than later, after getting beaten up by RJ Weston, Gabe Arnold and Jaxon Smith, when I wrestled great wrestlers I felt myself developing and could eventually get into shots on them. The movement and flow I was getting from them transitioned into my club, high school, and still to this day college matches. I started to believe the people who told me it was all worth it.

What role did your parents play in your wrestling? What did they do that helped or hurt your success/progress?

My parents always supported me. From putting the correct thing in the pantry when I was cutting weight or driving me to practice when I was younger. It not only benefited my lifestyle, but theirs at the same time.

When I was much younger my dad pushed me a lot to stay glued to the mat and would come to practice and talk to me about what I was doing wrong when it was the coach's job to do so. I did not enjoy that, especially because he wasn't a coach, but when I became a teen he really backed off and realized he could channel his passion in a different way. Once he made that transition and I had to rely on myself to get better and push myself, everything started to come together.

During my senior year, I wasn't sure I wanted to wrestle in college and my parents did a good job of not putting pressure on me to decide. I'm thankful that I was able to make that decision myself and it's made a big difference in my motivation level now that I'm on my own.

Any advice you would give to parents of wrestlers? Any advice to younger wrestlers?

The main advice I would give is positive motivation from parent to child. My dad preached to me that he didn't care what I did—whether it was cutting the grass, getting good grades, or wrestling—but he did care that I put 110% effort into everything I do. I carry that in my heart, mind, and body forever.

Caleb Henson

Age Started: 8

Youth Accomplishments: Average youth wrestler until seventh grade, then two-time state champion, and Super 32 finalist.

High School Accomplishments: Super 32 Champion, Fargo Champion, Flowrestling's Who's #1 Champion, three-time State Champion.

College: Wrestles at Div. I at Virginia Tech. As of this interview, Caleb is a true freshman, ranked No. 11 and just beat the second-ranked NCAA wrestler in the nation.

Did you have success when you started? When did you start to excel and what caused that?

I started in third grade. I didn't win a single match my first year wrestling. After a few years, I was okay, but nothing amazing. Before seventh grade, I only placed in state one time. I always wrestled hard, but didn't win a ton.

In seventh grade, I started attending practices at a club near where I lived. They ran practices out of a church and had a group of really good kids there. There were some parents who were organizing a group of kids to homeschool, so they could have a more focused wrestling training schedule. After I was there for about five to six practices, they said they needed another person to be part of it and asked me if I was interested. There were eight kids total including Kyle Golhoffer, Jaxon Smith and Caden McCrary (all Div. I wrestlers now).

Our daily schedule was:

- 8:00 - 8:30 am Bible study
- 8:30 - 10:30 am Online school
- 10:30 - 12:00 pm Practice with a private coach (Arturo Holmes)
- 12:00 - 1:00 pm Lunch
- 1:00 - 3:00 pm Online school
- 4:00 - 5:00 pm Strength training

A couple days a week, we would also practice at Woodland High School.

This lasted for two years and is when I really started seeing my first big gains. I was surrounded by wrestlers who were way above me skill-wise. I was getting my ass kicked for a while and then slowly adapted to the level of competition. I decided to quit football and baseball in seventh grade to focus on wrestling.

The other thing that made this situation unique is that there was no adult present. The pastor of the church was there, but he wasn't involved with what we were doing. We had to be accountable for ourselves. You had to want it. But everyone there wanted to be good so it was easy to feed off of everyone else's motivation and follow what they were doing.

The first big jump I could see in my wrestling was at Tulsa Nationals. In sixth grade, I was 1-2 and in seventh grade, I took second place.

This experience helped me learn early on what it takes to be great. I've always been a competitive person, but this group was all competitive kids so it forced me to up my game. We would have spike ball games end in a fight because it was that competitive.

I'm also not the most gifted wrestler so I knew I had to train to get faster, stronger, and better at wrestling just to catch up to others. I couldn't just rely on natural athleticism.

What role did your parents play in your wrestling? What did they do that helped or hurt your success/progress?

My dad was really hard on me when I was younger. He was never so bad that it made me want to quit or anything, but I definitely felt pressure. It did instill in me doing things at 100% though and it was ultimately a good thing.

Mom was always there for me for little things. She was big on proper nutrition and would make good, healthy meals. We always had healthy options at the house.

They were good about never forcing me to compete. It was always my decision. Sure, there were times I didn't want to go to practice. My dad didn't get mad, but he would give me a guilt trip sometimes and say "Okay, well, your competitors are going to practice." This made me realize others are getting ahead of me and I didn't like to lose, so it motivated me to go.

After matches, my mom was really good about not coddling me or giving me fake praise if I lost. She was consoling, but just accepted that it happened and helped me move forward. I was always really hard on myself and would beat myself up over losses, so she would let me take some time alone to deal with it. When I was in a better mood, she would just say "It's okay, you'll get back at it," and remind me there will be other matches. It was more about the future, learning from the loss, and moving on to whatever was next.

Any advice you would give to younger wrestlers?

When it gets hard, that's when you have to be great. Everyone's great when they aren't tired. Make yourself uncomfortable every day (i.e. ice bath, bike workout). Whatever workout you don't want to do is the exact thing you should do. Doing hard things is the best way to get better because it builds your mind and body.

I tell myself that I've earned the right to be here because I've done the hard things and I can fully believe in my training. I trust that I've done what it takes to win and not have second guesses.

What has been your "secret" to success? How have you jumped levels above what others (who also work hard) have been able to?

I've always been able to learn from everyone. Kids less experienced than me, coaches, etc. Everyone who wrestles has one thing they do well and I like to take from that and make it my own. From kids who are 0-2 at a tournament to the champ.

You can work hard, but it's also your lifestyle. Sleep, diet, etc. It all factors into the big picture. Practice is important, but it's also everything you do outside. Doing a little more than everyone in the room and staying after practice always made me feel like it gave me a mental edge. In high school, I made it a thing to stay after every practice to do 200 push-ups. I was willing to do more than everybody else.

I always had to find a new challenge. If I wasn't getting taken down in practice, I had to keep finding new partners who could beat me. In middle school, I wrestled with high schoolers. In high school, we tried to bring in college guys to work with. Getting mauled on is humbling and shows you there are levels to this. But it's also eye opening for knowing where you need to go. If someone beat me, I wouldn't be mad. I would embrace it and then go outwork that person every day to close the gap. This was with training partners as well as against people I may have lost to at tournaments.

I also like to turn little things into competitions in my head to keep pushing myself. I always loved playing games. For example, if we did sprints in practice, I always wanted to win the sprints. If we were doing stance and motion drills, I always pretended to be competing with others and moving feet faster and better than everyone else. Now in college, if we have a morning lift, I want to be more awake than everyone to conquer the workout. I mean yeah, it's easier to not be competitive…I just hate to lose at anything, even when I'm tired.

Recently, I've also been working on not looking forward to the end of hard things. Never look forward to the end of practice. Embrace each moment when you are in it and give it 100%.

Caleb Henson "I've earned the right to be here because I've done the hard things and I can fully believe in my training. I trust that I've done what it takes to win."

Jaxon Smith

Age Started: 5

Youth Accomplishments: Multiple-time state champion, multiple national championships.

High School Accomplishments: Three-time state champion (injured one year), fourth place Super 32, fourth place Fargo Cadet Freestyle All American, Cadet and Junior Freestyle World Team Trials All-American.

College: Junior World Freestyle Team Member at 92kg; fifth place at 2022 Freestyle World Championships; Redshirt freshman at University of Maryland and ranked No. 10 in the nation.

Did you have success when you started? When did you start to excel and what caused that?

I started at five years old. I got into it because the high school where I was zoned, South Paulding, had a basketball tryout for the youth feeder program. But when I was there, I saw a sign-up sheet for wrestling and thought that could be fun, so I tried wrestling the next day. I liked it immediately. I was pretty athletic as a kid so I picked it up quickly and was good early on. I was able to win most of my matches at local tournaments. About 10 to 11 years old is when we started trying to find higher-level events. Once I started traveling is when I got really good, but it didn't come right away. I went to USA Wrestling's folkstyle nationals and went 1-2. It was the first time I had lost in years and seeing that level of competition and how good the other kids were made me want to train harder. That's when I started wrestling year-round.

I was playing baseball and football at the time too. My dad

asked if I wanted to be good at three sports or great at one. He said he thought picking one would be in my best interest and he let me choose which sport. He was a big baseball guy so he probably wanted to see me play that, but more importantly, he wanted me to be great at something, so he let me pick. I'm competitive and driven by nature, so not wanting to be average is just something inside of me. I picked wrestling both because I was better at it, but because it was also more fun.

Tell me about ups, downs and emotions you felt along the way, as well as actions you took.

By 12 to 13 years old, I ended up being the No. 1 pound-for-pound youth wrestler in the nation. I hadn't lost in years and was the top-searched name on Trackwrestling. I got used to success and was at the pinnacle of the sport. But I was never the type of kid to look this kinda stuff up. I never looked at brackets or cared who anyone was. The only reason I knew I was the top-searched name on Trackwrestling was because kids at tournaments would say, "Whoa, you are Jaxon Smith".

But at the beginning of my eighth-grade season, I was in an awkward position and the ref didn't stop it. I ended up tearing my labrum and shoulder capsule. That took over a year to heal and come back from because I tried to do physical therapy first. I did about five months of PT and decided to have shoulder surgery. Then after only being back a little less than a year, I hurt my other shoulder in another funky position where my shoulder dislocated and did a full 360-degree rotation. I was out about eight months from this one.

During this time, I was really down on myself. The percentage chance of coming back from two surgeries and still being a high-level wrestler was low. This took an emotional toll on me. But eventually I tried to take a different perspective. The injury ended up being a good thing. I was working so hard that wrestling wasn't fun anymore. I was doing two practices a day, cardio, lifting and competing almost every weekend. Getting hurt allowed me to step back, refresh, and be grateful for the opportunities I have. It also allowed me to be a fan of wrestling, not just a competitor. The time off fired me up to be part of it again.

What role did your parents play in your wrestling? What did they do that helped or hurt your success/progress?

My parents had a huge role in my success. Even at eight years old, if I wanted to do a camp or tournament, they would always take me there and pay for it. New shoes, clothes, etc. they always supported what I wanted to do. My dad rarely ever missed a match.

When I was younger, between about five to 12 years old, my dad was strict on me. He set a standard for when I was older for how to think and taught me discipline and work ethic. He was very persistent about this when I was younger. He taught me about being schedule-oriented and having a routine.

Around eight or nine years old, each morning I did a 20-minute workout with exercises like push-ups, pull-ups, etc. He taught me that the morning started the discipline for the day. He told me "Nobody else is waking up to do push-ups and pull-ups like you." He would remind me that I was the only one doing it and it would pay off. A few times I wouldn't want to do it, but he would say "You don't have to be great, but these are things that great champions do." I believed what he said and I don't regret what he had me do for a second. One day when I was 12, I didn't want to go to a Sunday practice, so he made me watch a Michael Phelps documentary that talked about the best time to train is when you don't feel like it.

After the shoulder injuries a couple years later, I was struggling in my recovery process from my second surgery. I had just started working out again and my dad was pushing me to work hard. I was getting really frustrated with having to do the whole recovery process a second time, but mostly because I didn't think I could be as good as I used to be. I had a big breakdown and told him that I didn't want to wrestle anymore. After that he backed off and realized that if an athlete isn't self-motivated, there's not much the parent can do. The only result from being overbearing is to cause them to perform worse or quit. He understood I was self-motivated and realized he didn't need to push anymore.

Any advice you would give to parents of wrestlers? Any advice to younger wrestlers?

Parents: You can't make your kid want to wrestle. You can't make them want to be great at wrestling. They have to be the ones who want to be good and do the extra workouts and practices. It's just a different sport and takes much more internal drive than the other sports. The best thing to do is be there and support them for what they want to do. Help inspire them to want to be great. Help keep them accountable, but not so overbearing that it cripples them and makes them not want to wrestle.

Wrestlers: Be consistent and have fun with wrestling. If you want to be great, you have to be consistent.

Gabe Arnold

Age Started: 10

Youth Accomplishments: 12U national freestyle champion, third place Super 32 middle school division, three-time kids state champion.

High School Accomplishments: Cadet National Freestyle Champion, Ranked as high as No. 1 in the nation (winner of Flowrestling's Who's #1 event).

College: Currently a senior in high school committed to the University of Iowa.

Did you have success when you started? When did you start to excel and what caused that?

I first started wrestling when I was in kindergarten. I didn't like it at all. I got pinned every match in my first tournament and decided to quit right after that. My dad was a college wrestler, but he actually never wanted me to wrestle. Since I didn't enjoy it, he was fine with me not doing it. I decided that I liked other sports better at the time. In fourth grade, I decided to try it again. My dad was actually opening up his own wrestling club in Albany, Georgia, called Alpha Omega. Since he was doing that, I figured I would try wrestling again. My dad didn't really push me to get back into it. It just felt right and that it was something I should do.

When I started back, I did well. I won every local tournament that I entered. At state I went 2-2, but didn't place. But I felt like I had a great season. That spring, I was invited to be on a kindergarten through sixth grade dual team at AAU National Duals in Kingsport, Tennessee. I got my butt beat every match and didn't win a single one. The coach of that team felt bad so he got me an exhibition match with a kid from another team that was about the same or lower level than I was. I dominated him. But something about winning that match at a national event gave me a ton of confidence. In my mind, it completely erased the losing record and it made me feel that I could compete at a high level.

 Gabe Arnold "Winning that match at a national event gave me confidence. It made me feel that I could compete at a high level."

That same year (in October), I went to preseason nationals in Iowa. My dad was part of Team Georgia and they had organized taking some of the top middle school kids to this event like Nick Masters, Nicky Stonecheck, Charlie Darracott and Paul Watkins (all kids wrestling at a Div. I level today). I got to go there with all of those guys. Watching them compete was an eye opener for me. It inspired me to wrestle at their level. I ended up wrestling some of the best matches I had ever wrestled and took sixth. It was a great feeling to get on a national-level podium and I wanted more of that.

Tell me about ups, downs and emotions you felt along the way, as well as actions you took.

As I got better and better, we moved to Kennesaw, Georgia, and started training at Level Up. I was able to get great coaching, but also got my teeth kicked in every day by guys like RJ Weston, Caleb Henson, Jaxon Smith and Caden McCrary. These were all guys who have won major national tournaments. But while some days were tough emotional downs, I could tell it was making me better. I wasn't going down without a fight. They were gonna have to work for every point they got. Eventually I would start getting to a leg or snap them down to the mat, or even get a takedown. Seeing this progress really motivated me to stick with it. These were some of the highest moments I've had. Yeah, I just got my butt kicked for an hour, but I embraced getting that one takedown. I was able to take those little moments and turn them into big positives.

As I've improved, I set higher and higher goals. As a freshman in high school I beat some of the top-ranked seniors in the nation, only losing once that year. My confidence was sky high and I set a goal in 2021 to make a Cadet (17U) World Team. I was the favorite to win, but in one of the early matches I was thrown to my back and pinned. I was devastated and it took me a while to recover. This is an emotional sport and I put my heart into my training every day. I picture myself winning and expect to win every time I step on the mat so this really hurt.

After this, I just focused back on my training and set my sights on some new goals. I wanted to win Fargo (16U Nationals), get invited to Flowrestling's Who's #1 event and win the No. 1 ranking in the nation. I was able to accomplish all of these and I was back to having that feeling of being on top. But I think because I was on top, I lost my edge. I trained hard, but not above and beyond. I got a little complacent and it showed that whole next year. I lost some close matches during the season and

I let my weight get out of control. After all of this, I trained hard but my mind still wasn't right. I just couldn't shake the doubt I was feeling. As a result, I failed again at reaching my big goal of making a World Team. I knew at this point, I had to take some time off from competing and just focus on getting my mind right. After a few months of not worrying about competing, I came back and wrestled at a big event called Elite 8 Duals. I felt great and went undefeated, knocking off some top-10 ranked opponents. Right now I feel the best I've ever been.

So yeah, there are a lot of ups and downs that come with this sport, especially competing at a high level where there are expectations from yourself. But bouncing back and the feeling of overcoming adversity are what makes this sport great.

Did you ever think about quitting? If so, when was this, what caused it and why did you stick with it?

Absolutely. Multiple times. I tend to hold myself to a very high standard. So as a result, when I have had days where I'm getting my but kicked in practice, I tend to spiral downward. I have a hard time recovering and it makes me want to say "Screw this, I'm done." Having a good coach there helped me to gain perspective and push through the adversity.

This summer, after losing at World Team trials I had a rough time. Not reaching my goals really puts me in a bad head space. I'm such a goal-focused person and have high expectations for myself, so when I fall short it really hurts. It stings and it makes me just want to be done with the sport for a while. I didn't compete all summer. Part of me still wanted to and people were encouraging me to, but I also knew that I needed to just focus on training. I was able to go to the Olympic Training Center and train with all the junior- and senior-level World team members.

Even though I wanted to compete, taking time away and just training was one of the best things I could have done. I knew I needed to stop for a while and get to a point where nothing could phase me mentally. The best thing for my long-term development was to take a break. I'm about to enter into the grind of a college career, so there isn't going to be the opportunity to step away. I now feel great. My mind is solid and my wrestling is better than ever. I was able to take time for myself, not just Gabe the wrestler, but Gabe the person.

What role did your parents play in your wrestling? What did they do that helped or hurt your success/progress?

Early in my journey, my dad was always my coach and in my corner. When we moved to Kennesaw in sixth grade, there was a point where my dad realized he needed to separate the role of coach and dad. So when I started to train at Level Up, he took a big step back. I remember being at a tournament and there was a big match coming up. My dad was there and they were about to start but my coach wasn't there yet. My dad was like "I'll jump in the corner," and I said, "No, I'm gonna wait for my coach."

For my dad, this was a big moment but also a relief because he knew he could step back and just be dad. I think there's a big difference in roles that parents need to understand. My parents have done a good job letting the coaches coach and just being parents. They've never been those crazy parents at the wrestling tournaments. There's only so much time you have to be with your kids and if you spend most of that time getting mad at their wrestling, you miss those little moments of just being there to support them. You don't have to fix what they are doing or coach them. Just talk with them after matches without any stress. My parents did a great job at separating those roles.

Michael Kilic

Age Started: 6

Youth Accomplishments: Two-time Tulsa Preseason Nationals Champion, two-time Tulsa Nationals finalist, Super 32 middle school champion, several other major tournament wins.

High School Accomplishments: Three-time state champion; ranked as high as fifth in the nation; two-time NHSCA Champion, Cadet Greco national champion and freestyle All-American; Super 32 high school division third & sixth place

College: Freshman at Arizona State University (Div. I).

Did you have success when you started? When did you start to excel and what caused that?

My first few years I wasn't very good at all. I would get frustrated because each year my improvement was so slow. What caused me to reach a new level each year was a combination of 5 a.m. workouts with my dad and consistently going to practice.

Did you ever think about quitting? If so, when was this, what caused it and why did you stick with it?

I thought about quitting multiple times, but as I got better, I started to fall in love with the sport. This was in eighth grade. Before then I would do the work and I was getting good, but had a lot of ups and downs that made me frustrated and emotional. Sticking with wrestling and continuing to push on made me grateful, and made me want to get better each day. I used to get annoyed at my dad for getting me up so early to workout, but then when I was about 13 or 14 I started asking him to wake me up because I enjoyed the feeling of how I felt after each workout. The satisfaction of knowing I got better.

What role did your parents play in your wrestling? What did they do that helped or hurt your success/progress?

My parents played a huge role in my wrestling growing up. My dad was tough on me as a kid but as I grew older I realized that's exactly what I needed. Once I got to high school I was grateful for everything my dad had put me through because, although it was tough, it got me to the level I am today and taught me life lessons.

What I mean by "tough" isn't that he punished me all the time or was a jerk. It's more that my dad made me disciplined and pushed me to get better each day. I wasn't fully embracing the process, but when I did, I wanted to get better everyday. My dad and I would argue over the smallest things, but when I realized he was pushing me to become great and pushing me to be my best self, we became best friends. I developed a special bond with him through hours of work put in with him. He has always wanted what is best for me and when I saw that he became my idol and what I aspire to be as a person.

Any advice you would give to parents of wrestlers? Any advice to younger wrestlers?

My advice to parents is don't push your kid to a point where they are unhappy, miserable, and end up burned out. Let your kid make choices but also instill discipline so they understand why it's important to work hard. My advice to younger wrestlers is keep pushing. Don't quit. Stick it out because the lessons that wrestling teaches will stick with you your entire life and you will be grateful for all of it. I challenge you to get better day by day, not just in wrestling but as a human being. Be grateful for what you have because not everyone has the benefits of competing in a sport like wrestling. It will truly change your outlook on anything in life if you embrace the process.

Connor Weeks

Age Started: 12 but not serious until 14

Youth Accomplishments: None.

High School Accomplishments: One-time state placer (fourth), no national accomplishments.

College: NCAA Div. II qualifier as a sophomore at Belmont Abbey, ranked No. 7 going into junior year.

Did you have success when you started? When did you start to excel and what caused that?

I was definitely not good in the beginning but I started getting better in high school. I started really improving my senior year because I was healthy and was able to be consistent.

Tell about ups and downs and emotions you felt along the way, as well as actions you took.

I attempted some national events in eighth grade and my freshman year. I went to Super 32 and was 0-2. This was discouraging. I had cut a bunch of weight, worked really hard, and lost. But I was able to see all the mistakes I made along the way and learned from it. After time I had hindsight of learning lessons and it was ultimately a good thing. Because I was injured during my freshman high school season, my next national event was NHSCA Sophomore nationals. I was beating a good kid in the first round but then got pinned. I ended up going 1-2 and was very disappointed. I sulked and felt sorry for myself. But after a while I could look back on it. It was hard because I wasn't used to a tough national event where guys wrestled physically. After I got over the initial excuses and disappointment, I started to realize that I needed to be honest with myself. I needed to come to terms with what I did wrong and how to keep getting better. This wasn't something anyone did or said. I just had to be honest and realize that I wasn't mentally tough yet. Then I watched videos back to see technical mistakes and even see when I emotionally broke to figure out why.

What makes my journey unique is also that I had to deal with a lot of injuries in high school that slowed my progress. I tore my shoulder my freshman year and had surgery so it kept me off the mat for a while. During my sophomore year, I tore my ACL but wrestled through it. I didn't want to miss my junior season since it was so important to college recruiting. Unfortunately during that summer I ended up tearing my MCL also and had to have full reconstructive surgery. This really took a lot out of me mentally. All I wanted to do was wrestle and I couldn't. I had to find ways to stay engaged mentally in the sport, even if I couldn't do it physically.

I came back the summer before my senior year and that's

when I really started to see gains. For me, the "ups" weren't necessarily just winning. It was more that I was seeing progress (both in the wrestling room and matches). That made me really happy. I was executing moves I had learned. I could feel myself getting better versus top competition. Not just winning but moving better and reacting better.

But there were also some days of getting my ass beat in practice. This was initially discouraging. But then I went back to the process of taking accountability and solving the problem. "What do I need to do to get better?" Some days I would get beaten up so bad it was hard to see the progress and would think "Man I suck, why am I doing this if I'm not getting better?"

When those thoughts creep in, you have to force yourself to think about things that are also going well. Now that I'm older and more mature, I can think about being grateful and think about things that went well and that I did right. But also planning action for the things that need work. Asking that person that was beating me or a coach what I can do to get better in that position. This took time though. It takes practice thinking of the positive things. If you walk away from a bad practice and just chalk it up to sucking, you are gonna stew in negativity. Whereas forcing yourself to remember the good things will also help reinforce what you did right and not feel so bad.

Did you ever think about quitting? If so, when was this, what caused it and why did you stick with it?

Yes, in high school when I was going through really tough injuries. It was mentally painful, casting doubt that I wasn't meant for the sport. But pushing through and staying positive helped me get to a new level in college.

Some kids think about quitting because they think they aren't good or it's too hard. If you don't like it, it's okay not to do it. But if you do like it and are struggling to get better, my advice is to stick with it and eventually you will break through. I used to feel like an underdog wrestling in a crazy, tough room but stuck with it and it made me so much better. I had to fight not to feel sorry for myself being the underdog in the room.

What role did your parents play in your wrestling? What did they do that helped or hurt your success/progress?

My dad played a huge role in my not quitting when I was discouraged with injuries. If I talked about quitting, at first he said, "Okay, whatever you say," but he didn't believe me. He never pressured me to not quit. He just let me decide on my own. But I found out later that he called my coaches to get advice. My coaches then were able to get some older wrestlers that I respected to reach out to me and help me deal with the emotions I was feeling. I never knew that he did this until I was older.

My dad was never on top of me to go to practice or do extra. I was always self motivated and he was always happy if I was giving my best effort. He only got mad if I wasn't making a full effort. He never got mad if I lost. Since he didn't put pressure on me I wasn't scared to lose. I know others who quit because their parents were on them too much or got mad when they lost. He never damaged my progress. He always just supported me and let me drive the ship.

Any advice you would give to parents of wrestlers? Any advice to younger wrestlers?

Parents: Don't be so on top of your kid about wrestling. Encourage them to work hard and do their best but don't demean your kids if they are working their best. Take a step back and let the coaches coach. Just help keep them accountable to doing what their coaches say and that they are putting their best effort out there.

Wrestlers: Don't set your goals too low. Have long- and short-term goals. Focus on making progress more than looking too far ahead at big goals. One step at a time. But a lot of kids set their goals too low. Don't sell yourself short. I made that mistake in high school. Looking back I set my goals too low. Stay present and focus on the actions you are taking now to get to your goals.

75

David Panone

Age Started: 4

Youth Accomplishments: Nothing until middle school, then two-time kids state champion, Super 32 placer and NHSCA Champion.

High School Accomplishments: Three-time State Champion.

National Accomplishments: Fargo Cadet Nationals Greco All American, Grappler Fall Classic All American, NHSCA Senior All American.

College: Freshman at Div. II Belmont Abbey College.

Did you have success when you started? When did you start to excel and what caused that?

When I first started, I was not good at all. I only won three matches in my first three years and lost 59 of them. I struggled for a couple more years after that, even taking a year off when I was nine. When I decided to come back to wrestling, I had to learn that it's okay to be in a fight with the other person. Some kids are good at that, but if you aren't a natural fighter, you have to deal with overcoming fear and naturally avoiding conflict. At some point you just have to decide you want to be a winner.

Mirroring other people really helped. I looked at what the other "good wrestlers" were doing and how they acted. I tried to do things they did and feel like it seemed they felt.

I also think your outside life has 70% to do with it. When I started to get good, I had to "fake it until I made it." In life, I wasn't assertive and a confident person when I was younger. I had to learn to express confidence in myself and that translated into wrestling. If you are naturally confident outside of wrestling, it can be a big advantage starting out.

Tell about ups and downs and emotions you felt along the way, as well as actions you took.

I had to learn how to be okay with losing. When you are

young you get overcome with emotions and wrestling helps you channel those. I started out being mopey and losing made me not want to try. Or sometimes I would get pissed off. Learning how to process these emotions and being okay with losing is a big part of wrestling. If you look back and try to figure out why you lost, you can take actions to improve. You can make those emotional adjustments and technical adjustments.

There's also some pressure you feel as a wrestler, but it changes at different stages. When you aren't good, you may get pissed or sad, but you also feel helpless because it's not magical and winning doesn't happen overnight. I felt pressure when I was younger because I felt like everyone was better than me. It got WAY more fun when I started getting good. Even when I started going to national events and being on dual teams, I didn't really feel pressure. I wanted to show others around me that I was starting to get good. Once I started consistently winning at a national level, I had more expectations which did raise the pressure to succeed in higher level matches. You can also feel pressure from coaches because they expect you to win, but this can also be a good thing. It gives you the opportunity to communicate with the coach as to how to motivate you. Pressure isn't necessarily a bad thing if you focus it right.

Any advice you would give to parents of wrestlers? Any advice to younger wrestlers?

Parents: Let the wrestler learn their lesson without freaking out. Let them make mistakes and allow them to cool down on their own after a match and realize the mistake they may have made. Wrestlers with parents who got pissed when they lost were more focused on not making their parents mad than wrestling. This ultimately made their wrestling worse or led some of my friends to quit the sport.

My advice to parents would be to help the wrestler find their own motivation. They don't need a "motivational speech" or to be forced to work hard. There is a fine line between forcing someone and holding them accountable. Parents can also have a role in helping you be secure with yourself. Letting you make your own choices and understand the consequences of those choices helps you gain personal confidence which translates to wrestling.

 David Panone "Wrestlers with parents who got pissed when they lost were more focused on not making their parents mad. That made their wrestling worse."

For wrestlers:

• Learn how to fight. Even if you are getting your butt kicked, learning how to fight instead of feeling sad is huge. No matter how much you are losing, you have to know it will pay off and trust the process. Technique helps, but knowing how to fight is more important.

• Build confidence in one thing. You don't need to learn a lot. Just need to get good at one or two things. If you master those, you will build more confidence in yourself.

• There should be a mutual respect between wrestler and coach with an open line of communication. They should feel like they can talk to the coach, ask questions, etc. And if the wrestler doesn't feel there is mutual respect and a level of open communication, they either need to work at it on their end or it may not be the right coach. This should be similar with parents having an open line of communication and mutual respect.

Common Themes

Across each of these interviews, there seem to be a few common themes.

• While some find success early, most wrestlers have losing records early in their career. Even for the first two to three years or more.

- Many were frustrated early on with losing but stuck with it. If you like the sport and you feel like quitting, stick with it. It will eventually click.

- When it gets hard or when they are feeling bad about losing, they have to look back and figure out why. Solve the problem and take action.

- All of them sought out challenges as they moved through the process. They repeated the process of training, seeking the next challenge, facing adversity, then adapting to the next level by deliberately training to address the issues they faced.

- As they improve, you and others create expectations for winning. This can be motivating but also tough when you lose. It's best to let go of expectations and just wrestle your best each time.

- It's okay to take breaks every once in a while to get re-focused. Sometimes time away from the sport makes them grateful and intensifies motivation.

- More than winning, they wanted to see progress. Feeling like you are improving and getting closer to a goal is what keeps them going.

- Wanting your parents to be proud is a powerful emotion. If harnessed in a positive way, this can be very motivating. Thinking your parents are disappointed can be motivating too, but only to a certain point. If you are always expressing your disappointment in your child, they will feel like a disappointment and will ruin their self-confidence. It's a slippery slope that can easily ruin your relationship and end a wrestling career. Having an open line of communication can help you find the right balance.

- Being around other good wrestlers helped them mirror the attitude and behaviors it takes to be great.

- Every one of them was consistent with their training and did extra work on their own. This was either inspired by learning from other wrestlers, their own internal drive, or from their parents teaching them the value of discipline and having a daily routine at a young age.

- Parents pushed, but also learned when to back off. But they also knew their own kid's personality. Some are more self-motivated than others. Some need a push and some don't.
- When each wrestler took accountability for themselves, their progress skyrocketed.

Chapter 4. Why Some Wrestlers Quit

Of course, not every kid sticks it through until they have success and some who have success still quit the sport. If this is their first season, they have to at least complete it. After that they can decide if they like wrestling enough to continue. If they don't like wrestling, this is a very hard sport to be forced to do. I do not recommend making your kid wrestle if they don't like it. If they like it, but are struggling, then that's a different story and they should work hard to try to improve. It can take time. Having said that, this sport is not for everyone. Trying it for a couple of years and deciding it's not for you is not a bad thing. It doesn't make your child weak or a quitter.

Parents often are worried that their wrestler will quit or "burn out" so they avoid things that are too hard. They don't practice often enough, they wait too long before competing, they don't compete enough, they avoid moving out of the novice division or attempting more challenging tournaments. All of this is because they don't want their wrestler to lose and get discouraged. But as I've mentioned several times in this book, this fear is actually what is holding your wrestler back and can cause them to quit. In my experience, most parents who try to protect their kid from burnout have kids who never end up loving the sport or learn how to overcome adversity. They need to learn how to be comfortable being uncomfortable. They need to learn how to embrace taking risks, losing, failing, and how to use those experiences to improve.

At some point in a wrestler's career they may contemplate quitting the sport. Often this comes after a losing streak when they get into their own head. Usually at this point they just need to take a break and clear their mind. But there are multiple reasons wrestlers may quit the sport. Below are a few so that you can be prepared to address them and determine if the reason is legit or if it's something they just need to work through:

- **They genuinely don't like the sport** — They may be uncomfortable with the physicality, the pace of the sport is too fast for their brain to keep up, or they aren't very competitive. It may also be that they don't like how hard wrestling is. It's okay if they don't like the sport.

- **Some kids can't or aren't mature enough to handle the emotional aspect of losing** — This can manifest in two ways. They associate losing with being bad and why would they want to continue something they are bad at. But for some it's a deeper level of anxiety about competing. I've had a few kids who were naturals at the sport—even winning kids' state titles— get so freaked out before a match that they couldn't process the emotions. It would have been unhealthy for me to force them to wrestle.

I tried for months to help them get over this feeling and even tried a season where they only practiced and didn't compete, but ultimately this anxiety about one-on-one competition was too much for them. Quitting for this reason usually happens at a younger age (below 10) because they don't really even understand what they are feeling or how to communicate about it. It's hard to teach them a mental skill when they can't take a step back from it.

- **Your reactions to losing** — If their association with the sport is one with their parents constantly yelling at them or being disappointed in them, it doesn't make it very appealing to

82

continue.

- **Social pressure** — Sometimes if their friends don't wrestle and are part of a different sport, they will put pressure on them. They will say "wrestling is gay" and make fun of them for wearing a singlet. This is often a middle school issue and is tough to combat. Those who stuck with it despite this peer pressure usually had a strong group of friends in the wrestling community already. While wrestling is an individual sport, you can still make friends with people on your team or in your club. In fact, most wrestlers end up making friends with people they compete with.

Pivotal Ages

Over the years I have seen certain ages where it is more common that motivation fades, they consider quitting the sport and the journey in wrestling can take a different path.

Eight to Nine Years Old

If a wrestler started around five or six, this is often when they have had a full view of what wrestling is and they have decided if they are good enough to continue. If they lost a bunch the first couple years, and they don't think they are making progress, they will negotiate quitting the sport with their parents. In some cases, they may be right. Wrestling is not a sport for everyone. But sometimes they are making progress and just don't see it in the wins and losses.

If they enjoy the sport and you think they are truly improving, you should encourage them to continue. Maybe it's just that something needs to change. Maybe the training environment isn't focused enough or maybe they aren't going to the right tournaments. Sometimes it's just that they haven't decided what moves they like and once they own a move, they start finding success. Another option if they are struggling, but aren't ready to quit, is to practice only but not do tournaments. I know a few people who successfully did this. For whatever reason, the wrestler had a hard time with the pressure and emotions of matches and just needed a season to mature while still improving their skills.

They may also just need a season off. This is what we did with my son and it made a huge difference. Of course you run the risk of them deciding they don't want to return to the sport, but that may end up being what is best. Remember, you can't force them to want it.

Middle School

Seventh grade is usually when everything starts changing. Puberty is starting and they start finding their own voice. This is a very impressionable time in terms of finding their own identity.

As a parent you have to find a blend between guiding their behaviors and allowing them to find their path. Unfortunately this path may not include wrestling. This can be for a variety of reasons. It could be they have a group of friends who play basketball and they want to try it, or their friends make fun of wrestling because of wearing a singlet and rolling around with another person. I've also seen kids quit during middle school because of pressure that built up and negative experiences they had as a youth wrestler. They finally start getting the guts to say something or do something about it, so they pull away.

If wrestling is their path, this is the age to start giving them ownership over decisions and consequences for actions. They want independence so let them have some and let them build confidence from both failures and successes.

High School

If they stuck through middle school, there is a similar process that can happen in high school. This is when they really get tested and decide how much they want to sacrifice for their goals. If these were well-established early on, they should make it through the high school distractions. But many will succumb to the allure going out with friends, parties, etc.

I'm not saying those are bad things. They should have balance in their life. But there will be times they need to sacrifice those in order to train and they may decide those are more important. Most kids who wrestled when they were younger and make it through middle school will still stick with wrestling through the end of high school. It's more that they will decide how badly they want to reach their goals.

If they want to wrestle in college, they tend to be much more motivated. Those who know that senior year is the last time they will wrestle sometimes just coast when they finish out their career. But some will give everything they have knowing this is it. Some of this has to do with the culture of their high school team, but much of it is just the kids' personality and experiences they've had along the journey.

Burnout Myths and Realities

The concept of burnout applies to doing something that you want to do, but pushing too hard or too intensely makes you not want to do it anymore. While this can certainly happen, it's more often a fear than reality. It's usually not about training too hard or competing too much. There are many other factors at play.

You may have heard of the analogy of filling your tank or filling your cup. If not, basically this means that when your tank is full you have all the motivation and energy to give your best. There will be things that empty your tank in the normal course of expending energy such as practicing, competitions, etc. Along the way there will also be things that fill your tank, like praise from a coach or teammate, successfully executing what you have been working on, reading an inspirational story, having a good practice or winning a match. But sometimes you can empty your tank at a faster rate than it fills up. Do this for too long and eventually the tank will be empty and it's hard to continue, no matter how much you love the sport.

Here are the more common reasons I've seen the tank empty too fast and cause burnout:

• **Parents forcing competition and training instead of the wrestler owning the decision** – If you are being made to wrestle at a tournament, go to a camp or wrestle on a dual team and you don't want to, it can be miserable. You can do this a few times and deal with it; and sometimes kids just have to do things they don't want to. But when this is the norm and the wrestler doesn't buy into why it's important, they will eventually burn out.

Why? Because the motivation for high-intensity training and competition didn't come from within. They may not always decide what events to attend on their own, but they need to agree to it.

• **Losing without perspective** – Even the most mentally tough kid can handle only so many losses unless they have the right attitude toward them. Without the right perspective, if each tournament loss feels tragic and you don't feel like you are making progress, this can lead to a feeling of being burned out. This may be because they (or you) are focusing too much on results or they are on a massive losing streak.

Remember to help them focus on the process and the feeling of making progress. Remind them that progress is not linear and will have several ups and downs along the way.

• **Expectations (from them and you)** – Overly high expectations put more of the emphasis on results. Failing to meet expectations feels devastating and can be emotionally draining. Do this enough times and that emotional tank becomes empty.

• **Not allowing for recovery and strategic breaks (mental and physical)** – Sometimes when the tank gets too low it makes sense to take a week or so off. Or this may simply be one or two days off after a big competition. This is good for both the mind, but also to allow your body to heal. Taking time to focus on things other than wrestling can be very refreshing and allow the wrestler to come back fired up.

• **Cutting too much weight, too frequently or incorrectly** – This is a big one. If you are making big cuts every other weekend, this takes a toll. It's not only physically exhausting to train hard while dropping weight, it can be emotionally draining as well. Be strategic about which events you are cutting for and which ones it makes sense to wrestle your walk-around weight or only drop a few pounds. Also make sure the wrestler is not starving themselves of food or water.

• **Too much travel** – If you are flying or taking eight-hour car rides for wrestling events on a regular basis, this can drain the tank fast. This doesn't mean to not seek opportunities to find tough competition. Just balance your schedule, especially when they are younger.

• **Not having "fun"** – Wrestling should be enjoyable. The process of improving and the joy of competing should fill your tank. If wrestling is serious all the time, it ends up draining the tank instead. They should hang out with friends between matches, they should play games at practice, and they should be able to compete without pressure.

Chapter 5. Your Journey As a Parent

Being a wrestling parent is different from most sports. There can be some very complex feelings throughout the journey. Nervousness, excitement, fear, frustration, pressure, sadness, disappointment, embarrassment, and immense pride are just a few. And that's just during a single wrestling match. Most parents are wriggling up in the stands. Moms are clenching their hands together, or for some, yelling at the top of their lungs to "get up!" Dads are mimicking the wrestling moves in their seats. It's definitely a rollercoaster of lows and highs.

If you are a pretty laid-back parent, you may not be moving in your seat, but you may still feel many of these emotions inside. A lot of it has to do with the fact that you can't control how they wrestle. You are caught between empathizing how they are feeling, instinctively wanting to take away their pain, and wanting them to feel the joy of success. Or for some, you may feel your personal reputation as a parent is on the line if your wrestler loses or wins. You may subconsciously think others will judge you.

As they get further into their journey, there are stakes that come with winning or losing. This could be making the varsity lineup, qualifying or placing at state, or eventually college scholarships being on the line. All that time and money that was spent can feel like it boils down to a few single wrestling matches.

Eventually your wrestler will grow up and leave the house. You will want to have cherished the time you spent watching them wrestle.

Not only do these emotions get heightened during the wrestling match, you also know that actions off the mat can affect how they perform. Parents worry about their wrestler doing the right things like making weight, getting enough sleep, managing injuries, getting extra workouts, avoiding social distractions, balancing their grades, etc. Depending on your personality, you may be completely hands-off and it's totally up to your wrestler. Or, you may lean toward being a micromanager constantly hovering over them to make sure they are doing all the right things.

My word of advice? Breathe. Don't take it so seriously. It's just wrestling. In the beginning you may have some influence over their actions, but ultimately, if they want to be good at this sport it's up to them. They have to want it, they have to set the goals, they have to own the consequences of their actions. And that's why wrestling is such a great teacher of life lessons. As much as you may get caught up in the emotions of the sport, try to take a step back and allow yourself to enjoy it. Eventually your wrestler will grow up and leave the house. You will no longer be a wrestling parent and you will want to have cherished the time you spent watching them wrestle.

My Journey

My journey is a little unique because I was already a volunteer coach when my son started wrestling. I opened up my own training center and started coaching full-time when he started middle school. I think my journey provides a valuable perspective for all parents because I was so close to the process. I was fortunate to go through all the ups and downs at an intimate level and see my wrestler flourish at the end. I hope my story provides you both perspective and inspiration for some of the ups and downs you may go through on your journey.

The early years (4–10)

Because I was already going to practice three times a week, David asked if he could start going with me. His first experience in a wrestling room was when he was crawling in diapers during a private session I was giving and threw up all over the mat. At four years old, he said he wanted to start wrestling and I was very hesitant. I wasn't sure if he was ready, but he kept persisting and the excitement of him starting was too much for me. So he came to practices and the plan was just to see how he enjoyed it. He seemed to generally listen and pick things up, but he was tiny (37 pounds) and got beaten up a lot.

He then asked if he could do tournaments. I thought he was too young since the age group was six and under, but again he kept persisting. So I entered him in some tournaments. Luckily there were some kids in his weight class so he was able to get matches. I was nervous and excited at the same time. I didn't have any expectations since he was younger than everyone, but was hoping he would have fun. Luckily at his first tournament there was a kid similar to him and they just rolled around back and forth. I think David did get the first takedown but ultimately got pinned. I wasn't upset. Maybe a little disappointed for him since I was hoping he would like wrestling and winning would get him excited about it. But alas, that did not happen. He did have a couple close matches though (a 9-7 loss at his second tournament) and that was just enough to show me that he eventually could compete.

And yet, as you read earlier in the "Perspectives from the Wrestler's Journey" section, he was 3-59 his first three years of wrestling and lost 76 of his first 90 matches. It was brutal.

Most kids lose early, but then figure out how to win during

their second season. David would learn the moves in practice but would always collapse to his back in matches. In most of his matches, he would get pinned in the first 30 seconds. He was so cute though. He would be on his back, talking to the ref and telling them "I'm bridging! I'm trying to get off my back!" At almost every tournament, David would go 0-2.

Every once in a while he would have a great tournament draw and have a beginner first round. I would think, "Finally he has a chance of getting a win!" But then that kid would inevitably not show up and David would get a bye to the next round, leading him to wrestle a really tough wrestler. He would lose and then somehow get a bye again on the backside to pick up some other "hammer" (stud wrestler). The cycle continued weekend after weekend. And I would keep encouraging him weekend after weekend. He stuck with it and would keep learning in practice and show glimmers of progress, but ultimately couldn't figure out how to fight in matches.

When he was eight years old, he didn't place at any tournament, but was able to squeak out a couple wins at the state qualifier. The top four made it and David finished third. He went to state and won his first match! He then lost to the eventual champ and lost a close one the next round. Normally after he lost, he didn't show any emotion. This was the first time he cried. And while part of me was sad for him, in another sense I was happy that he actually cared enough to get emotional.

I'm not going to lie. It took an incredible amount of patience and optimism for me to keep encouraging him to stick with it. Other parents would say how they felt so bad for me since I was a wrestling coach and David would lose so much. I know that he probably didn't think he was ever going to be a good wrestler. But I kept seeing glimmers of him "getting it." Maybe I was just stubborn and didn't want to give up, but I felt like he just needed to keep trying and that I could coach him through it. I was still optimistic and kept just trying to improve little things

91

and encourage him that it just takes time.

When David was nine years old, the family was eating at our favorite Mexican restaurant and it was time for the season to start. I asked him if he wanted to wrestle. He wasn't sure. He kept going back and forth and I told him I was fine if he wanted to take a season off, but I also was still trying to motivate him to keep going.

Eventually my wife stepped in and made a decision. Clearly his heart wasn't into it, so she said no wrestling this season. I was disappointed but I understood. I didn't want to pressure him into it and make it my decision. If he was going to wrestle, he needed to decide for himself. So the season went on and I was still volunteering. I'm sure every once in a while I probably asked if he wanted to go to practice, but a season off is a season off. So I stopped and respected the decision and didn't bring it up again.

At the end of the season, only a few of our kids qualified for the state tournament. Two of them were David's size and it was brought up by the other coaches to see if David would be okay helping out to be a partner for them to get ready for state. I told them he probably wouldn't but would ask anyway. Both of them were David's buddies so when I asked, he was open to helping out. Surprisingly after all that time off the mat, David was pretty competitive with them and was scoring on them. He said he had fun. Well, when the state tournament rolled around, both of those wrestlers placed. When I told David, you could tell he lit up a bit and realized that if he was competitive with them, he might actually be good at wrestling after all.

He decided to return the next season. As a 10-year old at his first tournament, he was able to pick up two wins. He had three losses but two of them were close. We were making progress.

And then....he didn't place in the next four tournaments. The cycle continued. He was able to pick up a few wins, though, and that was enough fuel to keep him going. When we entered the Walton Raider Classic, David wanted to enter two weight classes so he could get more mat time. This was just a few minutes away from the house so the whole family came to watch.

At this point he had never placed in a tournament that was a bracket (he had gotten fourth out of five at a round robin, but that doesn't really count as "placing"). In the heavier bracket, he lost his first match, won his second and then lost again. In his true weight class, he was in a very tight, back and forth match. It really could have gone either way, but you could tell David was learning how to fight.

Tied 1-1, he got a takedown with maybe 30 seconds to go and had to ride out for the win. David won and I'm bursting with pride. Not because he won. He had won a few matches against less-experienced kids before. But I think this is the first one where he had to really fight and scrap to do it.

After the match, one of our other coaches told David, "Wow David. That was amazing. You just beat a stud!" You could tell David was excited. After that, he rode the momentum picking up a 7-0 victory in the semifinals. This was the most excited I'd ever been for his wrestling. Since he was four years old, David had never been in a semifinals match, much less place at a tournament. Now he was in the finals!

His opponent was a person who beat him 7-0 at the first tournament of the season two months before this. I was nervous and excited for him at the same time. You could tell David was excited too. This time, David was wrestling with confidence and you could tell. He right away got the first takedown and while there was a little back-and-forth, David pretty much controlled the match and won 6-2. This was the first tournament he'd ever placed in, and he won the whole thing.

The next three tournaments were back to a harsh dose of reality—DNP (did not place). He won a couple matches but ended up losing to one of the kids he beat at Walton. But then the state tournament rolled around.

David ended up winning his qualifier and was one of 24

wrestlers in his weight class. He had a bye in the first round and was able to win his first match. In the quarterfinals he had a kid we've never seen before. He was tough, but David wrestled great and gutted out a tough 1-0 victory and made it into the state semi-finals.

The next wrestler had beaten David handily before, but David had turned the corner now. It's a barnburner, but ended up losing 2-0. David wasn't fazed, though, and bounced back to win his conso-semis match in controlling fashion and is now officially a state placer! He ended up taking fourth. I was so incredibly proud of how he turned his wrestling around and stuck with it after all that adversity and all the losing. I'm not sure whether many kids could have stomached that, but he did. (Side note: the top four kids in that bracket all ended up becoming nationally ranked in high school).

Middle school

Once middle school hit, David kept grinding his way up and was able to find national-level success. There were lots of ups and downs, where he would find success locally and regionally, but then attempt a big national event and lose handily. There were times when losing would get to him, but he continued the process of competing, evaluating, learning and training specifically to improve strengths and weaknesses. There was no magic secret.

He just stayed consistent grinding up the ladder. He attended AAU National duals, VAC duals and other national events and made his way onto Team Minion whose team was consistently top five in the Gold Pool at team-based dual events. He had the opportunity to compete alongside and hang out with the best kids in the nation. Winning at a national level became more consistent (i.e. 7-1 at National Middle School Duals, 7-3 at VAC duals, eighth at Super 32 and winning NHSCA Nationals in 8th grade).

But this section is more about my journey and how I navigated when David was in middle school, including mistakes I made along the way. After things finally clicked, he decided that he wanted to wrestle year-round. I was already volunteer coaching freestyle and Greco, so that was an easy transition. He started going to a full-time training center with legendary coach, Arturo Holmes of The Wrestling Center, and started lifting weights more regularly. I took him to a gym that a former wrestler owned to do private sessions designed specifically for wrestling strength.

As they came up, I entered him into more challenging events, but I always asked him what he wanted to do. Did I influence this? Sure. I suggested what should be next if he wanted to keep improving and explained the benefits. But I never forced him to do these events. We always discussed it and it was his choice. Was he always super motivated to go practice? Of course not. I would love to say that after he placed at state, his hunger was insatiable and he devoured everything that was wrestling. David was motivated, would work hard and would always do what was asked of him. But he wasn't at home watching wrestling videos or doing push-ups in his room on his own. He may have gotten a burst of inspiration every once in a while, but he needed to be guided. As he got older, he took more things upon himself, but not as much in middle school.

I tried to find the balance between making sure he owned his training schedule and extra work, while also keeping him accountable and motivating him. I was always walking the thin, tight rope between being his father and being his coach. And let me tell you, that is a tricky balancing act with lots of stumbles.

I opened Level Up when David was in sixth grade, so he was consistently practicing three to four days a week. I also started running private sessions for him and a small group of his wrestling friends. Between the year-round wrestling, private wrestling sessions, lifting weights and starting to progress into more challenging events, David became a very skilled wrestler. He wasn't big (around 100 pounds) but he was strong for his size and he found some moves that he really started to own. He knew how he wanted to wrestle, always started matches fast and did not hesitate.

Now that David was finding success, while very exciting, something else happened. I started expecting him to win. Not that I expected him to win every match. It was more that when he entered a big tournament, there was more pressure to win and go deep. When they aren't very good, you're happy with any bit of success like scoring points or not giving up. However, when they start to win, this is the expectation.

The emotions become more complex the better they get. As a parent, when you've seen them wrestle at a high level, you expect that to be the case all the time. When it doesn't happen like this, you can get frustrated and even angry. You sacrificed time and money to travel to this big event, and it can be frustrating when they lose or, in your mind, they don't wrestle their best. You want the best for your child and you want to see them have success. But they are human and are going to make mistakes. You can't expect them to be perfect and wrestle perfectly all the time. It's easy to see all the things they "should have done" or "shouldn't have done" from the side of the mat.

I remember a couple of matches that stand out to me where I lost it. And honestly, I don't exactly know why I got so emotional. If you know me, I'm actually very calm. To set the stage, in David's seventh grade year he had won Southeast Regionals in both styles, so I was feeling really confident about his abilities. David made Team Georgia for Schoolboy (14U) freestyle/Greco national duals. We wrestled a team format versus the other states in the US and David got rocked. Like bad. He was 0-6 in Greco and 2-6 in freestyle. This was hard for me to see because he was just now starting to find success and the confidence was ripped right out from under him.

You start to question everything you are doing as a parent or wonder what he was doing wrong. Was he wrestling scared, not working hard enough in the room? It felt like it had to be something within his control, or maybe my control. What am I doing wrong? These are the things going through my head at the time.

After this, David entered the freestyle/Greco 14U national individual tournament. In his first match in Greco, David scored the first two points so I got excited. Then the other kid scored on him and got on top. He then wrapped his hand around David's body and hit a move called a gut wrench. If you don't know the Olympic styles, this basically means they lock their arms tight around the ribs and then drive their shoulder down to roll the opponent across their back for two points. It's not comfortable at all. David tried to fight off the first one and the kid scored, then (in my mind) David looked like he gave up. The kid rolled him over and over until he won 12-2 (the match ends via technical superiority in freestyle/Greco if up by 10 points).

I lost my shit. I mean I freaked out. Why? Because I assumed David just gave up and to me that wasn't acceptable. He came off the mat and I laid into him in front of everyone. I didn't care if people saw me because "no kid of mine was gonna be weak and quit on the mat." Looking back, I was an asshole. The reality is that I was embarrassed that David got beaten up. The other wrestlers I took to this event were all way more advanced than David was, so I guess subconsciously I wanted him to be like them. I wanted David to always dominate on the mat and how can that happen if he gives up? Did he give up? No. That kid had super long arms and had a tight as hell gut wrench. The more I coach, the more I realize how hard it is to stop the momentum of a move like that.

Plus, David had very little national-level Greco competition at that time. How could I have expected he was going to be able to easily stop that? So dumb on my part. At the time, I didn't see that all of these losses at duals and nationals were because of the level of competition he was facing. These kids were way more experienced and used to wrestling at a national level. I realize now that my frustration had built up because, after winning Southeast regionals, I had unrealistically high expectations.

After this, David was at a low point and said he wasn't enjoying wrestling anymore. He was beginning to doubt his abilities because of the long losing streak, but I know how I reacted at nationals was part of it as well. We talked about it and he took a few weeks off to evaluate things. He eventually returned and climbed back, having a great eighth grade year placing in Freestyle nationals, Super 32 and eventually winning NHSCA Nationals. It's amazing what bouncing back from adversity can do.

So what's the lesson here? For one, don't be an asshole to your kid when they step off the mat. Not only should you give them time to cool down over a loss, you should give yourself time also. Just walk away if you are frustrated. Talking to them immediately afterward will only end up with hurt feelings. Trust me, it's not productive. You don't need to analyze why they lost or things they need to do better. After you are both calm, then you can talk if you still think it's necessary.

The biggest lesson here is as a parent you need to reset your expectations as you jump levels. Just because they won locally doesn't mean they are going to win nationally. It doesn't mean they are going to lose either. It just means to approach each event with a fresh slate. Simply enjoy watching your son or daughter compete. This is their sport, not yours. Even if you are a coach, this is their journey. You don't have any control over what happens in their match. And I think that feeling of a lack of control is where a parent's anxiety and frustration comes from. There is nothing you can do. You can't wrestle for them. You can't prevent them from getting hurt or feeling sad if they lose. You really can only cheer them on.

High school

As high school began, I was nervous and excited at the same time. David had a goal of being a four-time state champ and that was not unrealistic. In eighth grade he had beaten all the kids that won high school state at 106 pounds, so in my mind, he could win it in ninth grade as well.

 You can't wrestle for them. You can't prevent them from getting hurt or feeling sad if they lose. You really can only cheer them on.

What was also refreshing to me was that he was finally going to have another coach. I had taken him to a couple other training centers before I opened Level Up, but I had been his main coach basically his whole life. This was the first time I could say "He's all yours." I knew he would be well taken care of since his coach had sent kids to Level Up and we already had a relationship. I was fairly able to let someone else coach him, and strongly desired that, because during middle school the natural struggle for independence began.

It wasn't that David and I had major conflicts over wrestling or anything, but you could tell my motivational speeches were starting to receive pushback. I really did try to let him decide his own training schedule and how much extra work he would do, but the days I thought he should be training I couldn't keep my mouth shut. I wouldn't harp on him necessarily, but I would throw in a passive-aggressive comment or two. "Oh, you aren't practicing today? It wouldn't be a bad idea to get some extra work in today since XYZ tournament is coming up."

I really tried hard to let him make his own decisions but in the back of my mind, the fear of him failing was too great. I wanted him to succeed and the coach in me wanted to guide him down a path of greatness. I wanted him to win the big tournaments, become ranked and go to some big Div. I college to wrestle. Whatever the pinnacle of success in the sport was, I wanted him to achieve it because I saw the potential in him. So when things weren't happening perfectly, the micromanager in me tried to step in to fix them.

When I tried to push more, he would push back. In my mind these were excuses or justifications for not doing every little thing right. In his mind, he's thinking "Why doesn't he trust me to do the right thing? I know what I'm doing and I'm working hard." And he's very similar to me. I don't like being told how to do things. I want to figure things out for myself. And I know myself. If someone tried to persist in micromanaging me, I would stubbornly shut down and not do it.

So during high school I learned the balance of truly letting go so David could own everything. For him to thrive in the long run, I needed to allow him to make decisions and face the consequences that come from them, both good and bad. I learned how to trust that he knew what he was supposed to do, while still being there to guide him when he needed it.

So...back to freshman year. David had a great season. He was 44-3 going into sectionals. At the end of the season, he had a decision to make. Keep cutting weight like he had been and stay at 113 or move up to 120 and wrestle the harder weight class. There was a point where the weight cut was miserable and his practices were not helping him get better. They were just weight cutting practices. So David decided to move up and try to take out a senior two-time state champion. This was a pretty bold move considering he was the favorite at 113, but David was willing to take the risk. And when he's decided he wants to do something, he typically does it. At sectionals, he ended up wrestling the senior in the semifinals and it was a brawl. A couple situations got dicey where he was almost put on his back, but David squeaked out a 4-2 win. He controlled his finals match against a really good junior and won 6-1.

Once at state, David took care of business in the first few rounds and earned his way into the finals. And not surprisingly, the senior two-timer also made the finals. In Georgia there has been a tradition for at least 30 years that when announcing the finalists, the lights shut down completely, spot lights come on and Phil Collins' "In the Air Tonight" starts playing. It is truly an iconic moment. I had been to the high school tournament in the past and there is such excitement when this moment happens. It gives everyone the chills.

For me, it has always been something even more visceral because I never made it to the state tournament as a wrestler. So when David's finalist walk out begins, the lights shut down and music starts…I begin to bawl. My knees buckled and in the words of Gabe Arnold, I began to "ugly cry." I couldn't help it. Years and years of effort. Knowing where David started from losing for so many years, to now being in the state finals as a freshman. I was overcome with emotion.

The match started and clearly the kid had a game plan for David. He was wrestling on one knee this time trying to avoid the shot David hit on him the week before. Little did they know, David had another weapon from there. When the wrestler reached for David's head, he hit a slide by. They squared up, but David was one step ahead and hit a knee pick on the far side. This was a "chain wrestling" series David had practiced and successfully hit before.

David got the takedown and rode him out the whole period. In the second, David was on bottom and this kid was cranking some nasty power halves. He was ripping David's shoulder off and the ref had to stop it a couple times for being potentially dangerous. David weathered the storm and in the third, the other kid took bottom. David is very good at riding legs, but also just so happens that this team is very good at defending legs. So this was gonna be a battle. For almost an entire two minutes, David was going for a ride. This kid was bucking, rolling and attempting to slip David off. But David remained calm, adjusted his position each time and when the clock finally ran out, David had slayed the senior and won his first state title.

I'm not going to chronicle every year of high school, but that beginning is significant to the overall journey I had as a parent. I was so proud of him and I knew he could continue to jump levels nationally. He ultimately finished as a three-time state champion, finishing third as a sophomore and was the winningest wrestler in school history (180-14 record) at Lassiter High School. He also placed at several big national events including Fargo and NHSCA nationals.

Did he win everything? No. But if you were to tell someone when he was nine years old and had a 13-76 record that he would end up a three-time high school state champion, they would say you were crazy. But this isn't about David. David is just an example of so many other kids in the same boat who lose early on in their wrestling career. As I write this book, David has graduated and is attending Belmont Abbey College, a Div. II wrestling program to continue his wrestling career. He loves the sport and is more dialed in than ever to keep improving.

So you tell me…does winning as a little kid matter?

Our College Recruiting Experience

If you have an older wrestler (or simply just want to keep reading), I wanted to capture some of my experiences as a parent during the process. This section is not a guide to the recruiting process, but if that is something you are interested in, you can download one at parents.levelupwrestling.com

For the offseason throughout high school, we did an annual cycle of the biggest national tournaments, mixing in some local and regional ones. I never made David wrestle in any of these tournaments—he always chose to. I suspect there were times he wanted to skip one or two. But even if he wanted to, he ultimately knew they were important for development and also if he wanted to wrestle in college. Performing well and knocking off a "ranked" opponent would catch the eye of a college coach and put him in a better position to be recruited. It turns out, this is much easier said than done.

David diligently wrestled each year at all the big ones (Super 32, NHSCA Nationals, Fargo, etc.). In each of these tournaments he would always wrestle well, often going deep but would lose in or close to the match before placing. He was able to knock off some ranked wrestlers and placed in some of the smaller national events. He was a sixth-place All-American in Greco at Cadet Nationals, which is a big accomplishment. But since college isn't Greco, it doesn't really do much for recruiting.

What I found out through the process is there are a ton of other really good wrestlers out there. College coaches are only proactively calling the top 5% of wrestlers. From 5% to 30%, it's all about relationships. The coaches David talked to and visits we took throughout the process were all from either emails his high school coach sent out or connections we had with other coaches.

For me, as a parent, this process was very hard. I was originally trained in sales and I know how important networking and proactively reaching out is. But this is a very awkward thing for a high school student to do. Since we were in the middle of Covid, there was an NCAA dead period where they couldn't do any face-to-face recruiting. This made the process exceptionally difficult. But also it caused me to put a lot of pressure on David. I knew the time would go by faster than we thought, so I wanted David to be reaching out to coaches on his own. I had him sit with another coach who has a lot of connections and they narrowed down a list of schools. They also talked about long-term goals and honestly, David wasn't really sure what he wanted. He knew he wanted to wrestle, but he also wasn't just going to say his goals were "to be a national champion and Olympic champion" like people think they are supposed to say. He was still figuring things out and trying to decide what you want out of life is a big task for a 17-year-old.

This is something I appreciated. He didn't want to just

do things that he thought others wanted him to do. He knew his choice of college would shape his life and wanted to be more thoughtful about it. But it also caused him to feel a lot of pressure. He knew a clock was ticking and he also felt the weight of performing well at these tournaments. I tried to not micromanage the process and constantly hound him about it, but I know he felt my anxiousness. At first he would change the subject or be short with his responses. But then he finally told my wife that I was getting on him too much about it.

Honestly, at the time, I don't know if I should have guided the process more or let it just unfold naturally. I know the pressure affected how he wrestled and how he trained. I know it caused stress between us. And had we not been restricted with Covid, we would have been able to do a lot more. There would have been more prospect camps, coaches could have talked to him at tournaments, and we could have brought more coaches to Level Up to meet the wrestlers. But at the end of it all, this was his journey and his path would have likely directed him to the same place.

Ultimately, David chose to wrestle at a small Div. II school called Belmont Abbey, right outside of Charlotte, N.C. One of my wrestlers goes there and was telling the coach about David. They reached out and David wanted to go for a visit to see what it was like. He wanted to keep an open mind about Div. I, Div. II and Div. III schools.

At first, I was very hesitant about this. My ego for some reason couldn't let go of thinking he should go Div. I. I mean, he had already beaten several kids who were ranked or even unranked, but wrestling Div. I. To me, I guess there was a little bit of a status thing. And to some degree, it was a reflection of me as a coach. I wanted to say, "My son, who I trained his whole life, who started his career losing and then dominated in high school, has chosen to go wrestle at _____."

But here's what I've learned throughout this process as a

104

parent. It's not about me. It's not my journey. It's his life and his wrestling and his life after wrestling. These are decisions that he needs to make. And it's not about status. None of that matters. It's about being in an environment and around people who will affect you positively in life. It's about making a decision based on long-term goals and what feels right. When he visited Belmont Abbey, he automatically clicked with everyone. It just felt right and I was very proud of his decision.

What I Learned As the Parent of a Wrestler

- **Patience and Optimism** — I learned first-hand that wrestling can take time. There are only a few prodigies out there and if you have one of them, appreciate that this is rare. Most kids lose the majority of their matches for the first couple of years. Help them recognize when they are making progress and don't feel like you have to point out all of their flaws. In the beginning there will be plenty. Even if it's going slowly, just keep finding ways to improve.

- **Proactivity and Ownership** — It's okay to lead the process when they are younger as long as they are bought in and want it. Just don't get so obsessive about it that it becomes your thing and not theirs. You can keep figuring out ways to help them improve in terms of training situations and competitions, but get them involved in learning how to improve on their own also.

- **Emotions** — It's easy to let the emotions of a match get to you. You are not in control of what happens out there so it manifests into trying to control it through yelling instructions or "encouragements." But these can come off the wrong way to your wrestler.

When he was younger, David once asked "Why are you yelling at me during my match?" In my mind, I wasn't yelling. But in reality, I was.

I was panicking because I didn't want to see him lose. Both

because of my own competitiveness but also because, as parents, we don't want to see our child sad. We want them to have success in whatever they do. You want so badly for them to grow up happy and confident and you think that losing an individual match could be devastating and hurt their confidence in the long run.

Fear drives this. Fear that they will grow up to be an unhappy, unconfident person who isn't successful in life. Or it's fear that if they lose, they will eventually quit the sport. Everyone wants their kid to be a winner, successful and happy so these emotions are powerful. What's the answer? You have to train yourself to relax and not get so caught up in the results of each individual match. Just enjoy that you get to watch your child do a sport they love. Just like a wrestler should, embrace losses as an opportunity to learn. If you need to, back away from the mat and make sure to hold your tongue. If they lose, just give them (and yourself) time to calm down. Let the coaches coach and just be there for them.

- **Help them find challenges, but at the right time** – Don't be complacent at the level they are. You are either moving forward or backward. I always made sure David knew that having tough partners in the room and seeking out new challenges was part of the process of improving. But this started around 10 or 11 years old when he started learning how to win. Before that, it was more about being persistent and just focusing on getting better at specific things. Once he started figuring it out, we started small. He didn't jump right into going to Tulsa Nationals or anything (in fact, we never wrestled there). David started out at some regional events, then progressed little by little. He moved his way up through the process each year and his progress was steady.

- **Learn how to let go** – This is not an easy thing. But it's something you have to progressively do as they get older and older. Specifically for wrestling, it's hard to watch them potentially lose matches knowing you could have helped them. This could be mismanaging their weight, not getting enough sleep or making sure they are training right. You have to learn how to trust that they will do the right things. Eventually they will graduate and have to do things on their own, so it is better to be there if they fail to help them learn. But if they love the sport and want to get better, it's amazing how much more dialed in they get the more you back off.

• **Start with a fresh slate of expectations as they jump into tougher competitions** – There are levels to this. And while they may be ready to compete at a higher level, it will also reveal their flaws. Ultimately that's a good thing. They can get away with stuff at a beginner or local level that they won't be able to as they hit better competition. So just approach each level excited to be there and ready to learn and adapt.

• **It's their journey, not yours** – Be there to support, help and guide them but not take it over or manipulate it. Let them find their own way.

• **Enjoy the process** – I was always told by older generations that it goes fast, and they were right. They will be out of the house before you know it. Love them and have fun watching them participate and grow from the sport of wrestling.

Section III
YOUR ROLE AS A
WRESTLING PARENT

At this point, you're probably thinking, "Donovan, you keep telling us to back off and let wrestling be their sport, not ours. Does that mean we shouldn't do anything?" The answer, of course, is no.

As I've mentioned in previous chapters, there is a strong correlation between active parents and successful wrestlers. Parents who are naturally competitive, or highly supportive, tend to have kids who are more involved. The kids who practice consistently, seek out challenging competitions and continuously find ways to improve are the ones who rise to the top. This mentality partially comes from genetics, as well as modeling their parents' behavior. So yes, parents *should* be involved. But there is a way to do it right and there is definitely a way to do it wrong. After reading this section, hopefully you will see the difference.

Parenting vs. Coaching

I won't be the first or the last person to suggest that parents should let the coaches coach and parents stick to parenting. But why is this? I promise—it's not because coaches want to reprogram your child's brain and you are getting in the way. It's because how kids respond to their parents is often an obstacle to them getting the most out of their training.

Rewind the clock a bit to when you were a kid (especially a

teenager). How did you feel about your parents constantly telling you what to do and how to do it? It's been happening since they were born. You have needed to provide them instructions for life and guide them through infancy, elementary ages, and so on. So every day, a kid has had a parent tell them what to do.

Usually around 10 years old the kid's brain starts becoming numb to their parent's voices. They want to think for themselves and, as they hit middle school, eventually tune the voices out. Maybe you recall Charlie Brown's teacher, "Wah, wah, wah wah, wahhh."

This is often why parents say to me, "Man, I just told him the same thing but when you say it, somehow he listens." I wouldn't take this personally. It's more that they see their coach as an authority figure in the subject and they see you as well… just their parent. You could be a world champion wrestler and it wouldn't matter. That is not your role to them.

As a result, it's important that the wrestling instruction comes from the coach. When the coach says it, the wrestler hears it as helpful advice. When the parent says it, especially if that parent wasn't a wrestler, all they hear is their parent getting on their case. The parent's focus then, should not be on trying to teach wrestling or pointing out all the things they did wrong, but on effort and attitude.

Don't Board the Helicopter

Depending how seriously they decide to take wrestling, your primary role may simply be driving them to practice. As they decide to get more serious and take it to another level, your role will evolve. Section III contains perspectives and will explore tools you can utilize to support them.

For some personality types, however, it can be very tempting to want to apply these tools and micromanage your wrestler's career. Avoid becoming a "helicopter parent" (constantly hovering overhead and attempting to oversee every aspect of their life, including their wrestling). This type of control will make them want to quit the sport and limit their long-term development.

I will continue to reiterate how important it is for them to learn how to take ownership and full responsibility for their own improvement. Micromanaging prevents them from taking responsibility. Instead of doing everything for them or telling them everything to do, your role is to help support them in achieving their goals.

When your kids are younger, they need more guidance. Up until about eight years old, they are relying on you to tell them what to do and how it needs to be done. Starting around age eight (or earlier with some kids) is when it's time to start putting things on them and help them develop a good work ethic and habits. Give them more tasks to accomplish on their own so they build confidence in their ability to make good decisions and take actions, not simply on doing what they are told. Even if you know they will mess it up, you will be there to help them learn.

Gradually, as they accomplish tasks on their own, there will be a sense of pride. From a wrestling perspective, this might mean coming up with daily workouts at home, like pull-ups and push-ups. Maybe put a chart of the fridge for them to check off when they finish the workout. They can even set goals for how many they can do in a row or in total and write down their progress each day.

 It is important for them to learn how to take ownership for their improvement. Micromanaging prevents them from taking responsibility.

Another way to foster responsibility and self-discipline is to take their input on decisions. This could be what their practice schedule is going to be, what tournaments they want to wrestle in, what food to buy at the store, etc. Even if you are not giving them a choice, collaborate with them and guide them down a path to make them feel like they have buy-in.

Once puberty starts taking hold you have to learn how to pull back and let them take more of the reins. They will inevitably fight for their independence, so it's a great opportunity for you to decide what actions you are comfortable with them taking.

In wrestling we are asking them to take risks like attempting a takedown. If they are successful, this will build confidence and trust in their abilities. If they mess it up, they now have the opportunity to evaluate what happened, learn, practice, and make another attempt. Once they get the takedown, this builds confidence in both the skill and the process they took to master it. So allowing them to take risks in their decision making is no different. There are natural consequences for their actions or inactions that they will learn from.

A wrestling example might be allowing them to make decisions on how to make weight. You may have guided them on how to eat healthy at first. Now they know what they are supposed to do. You don't need to micromanage them on what to eat. Buy good choices for the house, but if they choose to eat poorly or not drink enough water, the natural consequences are feeling horrible when they practice and possibly missing weight. That's on them.

I know you're afraid they are going to make a mistake or do something wrong that will ruin their wrestling career. Trust me, I know the feeling. This is the draw towards nagging and making sure they are doing all the right things. But allowing them the opportunity to make these mistakes and have it sting a little bit is a huge part of learning not just as a wrestler, but as a human. Then they can figure out what went wrong and make the adjustments.

You can be there to guide them and help them brainstorm what went wrong, or where to ask their coach for help. In fact, much of the direction they get for their wrestling career should be from their coach. Instead of trying to solve everything yourself, direct your wrestler to ask their coach for advice.

Chapter 6. Supporting Your Wrestler's Journey

Along their journey you will need to make decisions on how to support them. Understand how serious your wrestler wants to take the sport and how much you will need to be involved. This may also change over time as they get older and more experienced. If they want to achieve success at the highest levels, it will take a high level of dedication not just on their own, but from you as well.

Decisions along the way may include the best training location, how often to practice, what tournaments to attend, and additional resources you may need to provide that will help them reach their goals. Below are some tips based on my experiences as a coach and parent:

Decisions About Training and Competing

In the beginning, this can be simple. Find a club nearby or join the school's team and follow whatever competition schedule they put out. But as your wrestler becomes more serious about the sport, you will need to make decisions that help them progress and continue to be challenged.

School program vs. club team vs. full-time training center

It used to be that all youth wrestling programs ran through volunteer-coached school programs or possibly even an after-school team coached by a teacher. Nowadays, depending on where you live, you may have access to a full-time training center.

Where your wrestler should train depends on multiple factors. Where you live, your wrestler's experience, quality of coaching, your wrestler's goals, and your judgment as a parent. If they are just starting out, find a program where they can feel comfortable and develop a joy for wrestling first.

I run a full-time training center, but I often tell parents of new youth wrestlers to start at the school feeder programs. In most areas of Georgia, there are USA Wrestling club programs that feed into the high school where they will attend. I think it's better for them to get a season under their belt first and decide whether they like wrestling before coming to me.

With that in mind, you can also start at a full-time training center as well. Many training centers, including my own, have beginner programs. If your wrestler is younger, in the first year or two, just focus on finding a place where they will learn good habits, but don't take it too seriously. If your wrestler does show a hunger and an aptitude for the sport, find a situation where there is a full-time coach and tougher partners. This may even just be supplemental, outside of your regular practices. If they are motivated to improve, they will adapt to their surroundings. There may be tough days for sure, but as long as they are resilient and keep working to improve, this environment will help them jump levels.

Consistent coaching

I do believe that as a wrestler improves, they should be seeking out tougher training partners. At the same time, I firmly believe that they need consistency as well. They need a coach whom they can connect with on an emotional level, and who understands what makes them tick.

Kids who hop from room to room tend to isolate themselves from everyone. The parents justify it with finding partners and getting a "variety of coaching," but they don't have the same experience of camaraderie with other wrestlers. There isn't the same bond with others who are all working toward the same goals and go out of the way to help each other. They will also isolate themselves from having coaches who are fully bought into helping them on all levels (technical, mental, physical).

That said, if you are in a bad situation, that's a different subject. You should leave a toxic environment. Or it also makes sense to leave if you have graduated past the beginner level and need to find a more advanced training environment.

If, however, you've found yourself a balance of good coaching and solid training partners, I believe that's where you should spend the majority of the time. Then, periodically it can be beneficial to visit other places or attend camps to wrestle with new partners or get input from a different coach. If this is the case, talk with your primary coach first so they can be in the loop. A good coach will embrace this and also wants you to gain new perspectives.

Should you start private lessons?

Private sessions can be individual, with a partner or with a small group of four to six at most. The biggest benefit of these is the personal attention of detailed instruction tailored to the wrestler's strengths and weaknesses. Some kids simply learn better in an environment with fewer distractions.

As someone who does private sessions for up to 20 wrestlers per week, I've seen some patterns as to who will get the most out of them. My opinion is that you shouldn't start private lessons until they have wrestled a full season, or at least a few months if they started in the off-season.

Their brain needs to feel what wrestling feels like first, make mistakes, try to determine the solution and then want to seek to find the answers. When you program someone "perfectly" from the beginning and the match doesn't go according to script, they tend to freeze up.

I also fully believe that in order for a private session to have its maximum impact, the wrestler needs to be the one seeking the answers. They need to be hungry and motivated. I've had some miserable private sessions where the kid wasn't making any progress for months. I would later find out their parents were making them go and they didn't even want to wrestle. Wrestling is too hard of a sport to be forced into it. I do think private sessions can be instrumental in a wrestler's development, so if you think it's something your wrestler may want to do, talk to them first and get their buy-in. However, if private sessions are only happening because of your initiative, you are likely wasting time and money.

When should you wrestle year-round?

This is a very individualized decision. I do believe that when they are young, kids should try a bunch of different sports, as well as non-athletic activities. This way they can decide what they enjoy and have an aptitude for.

The parents of an eight-year old who have already decided their kid is going "year-round" in any sport can cause their child to lose interest and fade out as they get older. On the opposite side of the spectrum, I don't think you should force a kid to play three other sports when they already know what they want to focus on. Every situation is different and depends on each kid's specific interests and hunger.

In my own experience, middle school is when they start developing their identity and put labels on themselves. "I'm a wrestler, I'm a soccer player, etc." They identify with a "tribe" of others like them. Some kids, even younger kids, just know they are wrestlers. But I still think they should be open to trying other sports.

This doesn't always have to be team sports like football or baseball. Other sports and activities like swimming, gymnastics, rock climbing, or even "ninja warrior" build complementary skills to wrestling such as grip and core strength. Whatever they try, the decision to train year-round needs to be theirs.

In wrestling, it often happens organically. They may decide to do freestyle/Greco instead of playing a spring sport. Or they start training in the fall to get ready for folkstyle season. My son didn't start wrestling freestyle until 10 years old. I suggested it, but he still decided he wanted to do it. At the time he was also swimming and, from ages five to 10, he tried soccer, baseball, and football. Eventually he chose to stop swimming at 12 years old. He decided on his own that he liked wrestling better. This commitment narrowed his focus and certainly correlated to when he started making huge gains.

Taking breaks

Whether they train year round or just during wrestling season, it's important to understand when to take strategic breaks. While the "No Days Off" mantra is noble, I think it gets misinterpreted. Your muscles and your mind get stronger during the rest period between workouts, not during the workout itself. Without recovery, your body just gets worn down and can't perform at its best. This doesn't mean they should take a break just because they are tired and want an excuse to skip practice. But it means devising a training and competition schedule that includes small mini-breaks or recovery days in order to keep training hard.

I do think it takes an obsessive desire to be great at something but you should be obsessive about constant improvement and understanding the process to be great, which includes strategic breaks. There will always be a new tournament coming up. You have to decide which ones are important. Again, it goes back to their hunger and how they respond mentally to wins and losses. If they are on a winning streak, it can be good to feed the momentum and keep competing. If they are on a losing streak, it may be time to take a break from competing and just focus on training.

Much of this will also be wrestler dependent. Sometimes, bouncing back from a hard weekend is the right decision too. Wrestlers often have their best gains right after big adversity. As an example, one of my wrestlers attended a big event called NHSCA nationals. She did not wrestle up to her potential and mentally broke in a couple of her matches. She had been signed up to wrestle in the World Team Trials in a little over a month (which basically means you are attempting to be the No. 1 wrestler in the nation to represent Team USA at Worlds). Her parents talked about her not wrestling at trials because she wasn't wrestling well and maybe she wasn't ready. I told them that I would talk to her and decide.

She decided that one month was enough time to clean up some of the issues she was having both with her wrestling as well as her mindset. Because she made this decision, she buckled down and reset herself mentally. She let go of the pressure and expectation of performing at a national event and just tried to focus on improving her wrestling. As a result, she ended up wrestling one of the best tournaments of her life and lost a close match in the semifinals to the eventual champion. She took third place, which qualified her to be on Team USA.

The takeaway here is that taking a break and not competing is going to be a case-by-case basis. As a general rule, I usually tell kids who wrestle year-round to take one to two days off after a big weekend tournament and one to two weeks off after a long training cycle for major national events.

Your wrestler doesn't have to wrestle in every event, but plan out a schedule with them that makes sense for progressively challenging mat time. Be prepared to make a judgment call if you are feeling the momentum and want to do more or need to pull back a bit. With this in mind, don't avoid an event just because it's hard or are worried about losing. If you've decided it's the right time for a challenge, then embrace it and put everything you have into it.

National tournaments and dual events

Once your wrestler becomes more committed to wrestling, it may be time to start hitting regional and national events. Nowadays there is a "national" event almost every other week somewhere. I purposefully put national in quotes because many of these end up just getting kids around the region. This doesn't mean these events aren't worth attending, but do your homework on the quality and quantity of people who have attended previously.

If they are new to travel, these smaller events are a good introduction since they typically don't have as many "hammers." But it's easy to get caught up hitting all of these events. It's important to space out which and how many major events you attend. Too much travel and too many back-to-back weight cuts is a big cause of burnout. You'll also have to figure out what you can afford. But assuming your wrestler is hungry and wants to improve, seeking out tough competition is vital to continuing their development. If you can find that locally or within a short drive, then that's great.

Over time, as they improve, hitting some of the bigger regional and national events is an important next step, depending on their age and experience level. I've seen several parents jump in way too soon and others hold back too much thinking they are not ready. Readiness is subjective—varying from wrestler to wrestler—and you should talk with their coach to get their opinion.

My perspective is that generally they should wrestle at a local level for at least two to three seasons. If they are placing and winning tournaments consistently, then you can start dabbling in travel and see how they do. It's not just about their record—they need to be competitive and show progress. How are they reacting? Are they coming back with a desire to train harder? Did they have fun regardless of winning or losing? Did they seem to learn and make progress? If so, they are probably ready for more.

On the other hand, if they are getting in their own head too much and compounding losses are causing them to doubt themselves and regress in their wrestling, then it may be time to pull back and focus more locally to build the confidence back up. Remember, however, that while elementary-age events are fun, they are not very important in the grand scheme of things.

Kindergarten to fourth grade is not the time to get overly excited about how talented your wrestler is and have them travel nationwide. Be very selective of the events you go to at that age. Once they're in fifth and sixth grade, they can start hitting a few more and then, by seventh and eighth grade (assuming they are ready), they should get in as much as possible to prepare for high school.

Developing good habits and putting in extra work

A big part of your role is teaching them good habits from a young age. The younger you can start these and just make it part of their daily routine, the more it will stick when they are older. Not only are these helpful to wrestling and other sports, they are also great habits for life.

Recovery

Greater attention has been paid lately for how important recovery is for optimal athletic performance. When kids are young, they tend to recover more quickly naturally, but it's important to teach these habits for later in life. As puberty sets in, understanding how to properly recover is very important. It not only gives your wrestler a competitive edge by improving how much energy and mobility they have in practice and competitions, it also prevents injuries. The good news is that the most effective methods of recovery just happen to be free! These include sleep, water and stretching. But it's also a matter of creating good habits and doing it right.

Quality Sleep

Not only is this the biggest factor in recovery, being well-rested helps athletic performance, injury prevention, academics and life in general. How can you influence this as a parent? Investing in a good mattress is the easiest thing you can do.

Many times, parents get the good mattress, leaving kids with tattered hand-me-downs from the old apartment. Studies show that sleep quality can improve by as much as 62% simply by switching mattresses. You can also ensure their room is a conducive environment by fully covering the windows so that extra light does not disturb their sleep. According to the Sleep Foundation, kids ages six to 12 need nine to 11 hours of sleep and adolescent athletes need nine to 10.

While it can be tough to enforce this as they get older, you should start teaching good habits at a young age for bed times, as well as limiting screen time one hour before bed. This can be simply done by not putting a television in their room and requiring all phones to be left in a common family room before going to sleep. At a minimum, you can use parental controls to turn their phone off at a certain time. If their schedule allows for it, a 15-minute power nap right after school can be a huge boost in their ability to get homework done and have energy for a quality practice.

If you want to read more about how sleep can affect athletic performance, visit https://www.sleepfoundation.org/teens-and-sleep/student-athletes-sleep-time

Drink lots of water

According to Children's Health Care, to maintain optimal hydration throughout the day, young athletes should drink ½ to 1 ounce of water per pound of body weight. If we translate this into 16-ounce water bottles, this would be 2 ½ to five bottles for a day for an 80-pound wrestler, or five to 10 bottles a day at 160 pounds. Drinking a bottle a couple hours before practice and, of course during practice, will help ensure optimal hydration.

Post-practice routine

After practice the muscles will be worn and will tighten up. The key spots for wrestlers are hips, hamstrings, glutes and lower back, as well as the shoulders and neck. Have them do a simple five- to 10-minute stretch routine immediately after practice. When you get home, have them spend five minutes using a foam roller, lacrosse ball or percussion massager (i.e. Theragun) on the low back, glutes, thighs, hips, hamstrings and upper back/ shoulders. This will prevent the facia (layer of tissue over the muscles) from tightening up and thus limiting oxygenated blood flow necessary to help the muscles recover. As they get into high school and higher levels of national competition, they should also consider utilizing saunas and ice baths prior to big events in order to reduce inflammation. But this is for the serious, committed athlete only. Ice baths are no joke.

There are other methods for minor injuries as well. In addition to the basic use of ice, there are also new methods when things get really bound up and affect their ability to train. Dry needling by a physical therapist is very effective to pinpoint specific trouble trigger points. Cryotherapy centers are popping up in many places and report to aid in recovery and reducing inflammation. And of course chiropractors focus on spinal and skeletal alignment. I would suggest doing your own research to see if these methods make sense for your wrestler.

Nutrition

The simplest thing you can do as a parent is to make sure that healthy choices are available. If junk food is around, don't be shocked when they eat it, especially if they are supposed to be managing their weight. Early on, teach them how to prepare a healthy snack or meal on their own without always needing you. If you want to reduce the barrier of preparation, simply pre-cut and bag snacks for on the go.

Good nutrition is also a big factor in recovery, as well as having energy for tough practices. To keep it simple, each meal should include a source of protein, complex carbs and a vegetable or fruit. The cleaner, the better. Processed and fast foods, while convenient, are unhealthy and can leave them feeling sluggish.

They should also have a pre-practice snack to provide optimal energy. When I've had wrestlers become light-headed during practice, the first thing I ask is when they last ate. It was usually their school lunch around 11 a.m. Better energy equals better practice, which leads to more confidence. I'm a big fan of apples and bananas, but also a simple (but not sugary) snack bar can help too.

Nutrition during tournaments is important as well. Keep it simple and make sure they don't over-indulge after weigh-ins. This can lead to being too full and wrestling sluggish. A few suggestions are bagels with peanut butter, nuts, as well as fruits such as grapes, cut-up apples or bananas. Avoid sugary snacks since those will lead to an energy crash during matches.

If they are an older wrestler and need to manage their weight or cut weight for a big event, there are more involved steps to doing it right. Most wrestlers do this wrong and end up starving themselves or getting dehydrated. To help with this, I've created "The Dummies Guide to Making Weight," which can be downloaded at parents.levelupwrestling.com.

Strength Workouts

Strength can be an advantage in wrestling, especially at an early age. And while the capacity to gain strength when younger is somewhat limited, learning how to properly work out is very important. Not only do they develop stronger connective tissue, they also develop more muscular control, good form and prevent injuries.

While I know some parents who hoard workout equipment in their basement, you don't need a lot to get an effective workout. It can be as simple and inexpensive as just using body weight. To me, the most important investment is a pull-up bar. This hits a lot of areas related to wrestling. Grip strength and endurance, shoulders, back and core strength. If you are able to, start your wrestler creating good habits early in their career.

These workouts can be scheduled when they wake up, right after practice or before they go to bed. Some grouping of pull-ups, push-ups, and core strength. I also recommend setting a goal and marking it off from a checklist each day.

If you have the ability to provide more equipment at home or go to a gym, make sure they have a consistent routine. One resource I would recommend is Coach Dustin Myers from Ohio. He is the Ohio Regional Training Center strength coach and has created several guides for kids of all ages. You can find his e-books at https://oldschoolgym.com/collections/e-books.

If you have the means, going to a dedicated strength or sports performance center can also be helpful. I've had some wrestlers make big gains doing this, not just because they are experts in sports performance, but also the weekly sessions force them into a regular routine.

Mindset Training

A newer field in sports performance is mindset training, also called sports psychology. The mental game is a huge part of sports and one could argue the biggest factor in reaching the

123

highest levels. Just like the other skills of technique, strength, and speed, some kids naturally are gifted here and some need more training.

Some wrestling coaches are very good at helping their wrestlers through these challenges and these are also skills they can research online and develop on their own. It may also make sense to pay for a specialized service to help such as Wrestling Mindset or another sports psychologist. What exactly do I mean by "mindset training"? Examples are:

- Developing a pre-match routine to get in and stay in the zone
- Dealing with nerves
- How to refocus when matches get out of control
- Perfectionism and overthinking/ hesitation during matches
- Anger or depression issues when losing
- Choking in big matches

When they are younger, you are basically their mindset coach helping them deal with losing and nerves. Much of this book is about how the role of the wrestling parent affects their wrestler's mindset and ways you can help. As they get older or they get into higher levels of competition, these skills may need more specific professional development and there are resources out there that can help if you feel it makes sense.

Patterns of Successful Wrestling Parents

I always wondered if there was something that parents of the "good wrestlers" were doing differently. Over time, I've observed that there are definitely common characteristics and actions of these parents. There are no guarantees, and plenty of wrestlers have found success despite not having parents with these traits, but it certainly can't hurt to put your best effort forward.

Also, when I say successful, I mean the wrestler makes

continuous progress while enjoying the sport (and keeping their relationship with their parents intact). Yes, they win and win at high levels. What's most important is not how quickly they find success, but rather that they eventually do.

Below are the most common traits parents of successful wrestlers exhibit:

1. They actively find ways to help their wrestlers improve – They consistently take them to practice, seek good coaches and training partners, and actively take them to tournaments and camps to get mat time. They are always finding new challenges to keep them forging ahead.

2. They teach them about drive, commitment, and sacrifice by doing it themselves – Driven parents are willing to travel, adjust their schedule to make practices, and sacrifice their weekends to be on the mat. They also demonstrate these traits in their own work and personal life, thus leading by example.

3. They find a balance between positive and negative motivation – Each child is different as to what motivates them, but you can push them to be their best and be positive at the same time. Being positive doesn't mean coddling or praising them for things you expect, but it does mean recognizing when you are proud of an accomplishment or their hard work. Yes, there are some eight-year-old studs whose parents constantly berate them, but that motivation is short-term. They win matches to avoid getting yelled at, not because they love the sport. The ones with parents who find a balance between pushing them and building their confidence are the ones who find long-term success.

4. They hold them accountable – When wrestlers are younger, you tell them what to do. As they get older, they need to own the training and find the motivation from within in order to achieve new levels. Successful wrestling parents help to keep them focused while also giving them space to fail and learn on their own.

5. They do not tolerate bad behavior – Nobody likes to lose. However, if their wrestler throws a fit on the mat, the parent addresses it immediately or takes them home.

6. They help them bounce back – Part of wrestling (and life) is learning how to fight through adversity. Successful wrestling parents don't tolerate excuses like "I'm tired," "my stomach hurts," or "I don't feel like it." Wrestling is a tough sport and kids need to learn how to do hard things—that they CAN do hard things.

7. They understand the role of parent versus coach – They allow the coach to do the coaching and they focus on the parenting. They don't criticize their wrestler in the car after practice and they don't tell them things they need to be doing after a match. Instead they concentrate on addressing things like working hard, not giving up, and being a good competitor.

8. They know when to take breaks and back off – The best wrestling parents sense when it's time to take some time off or if they are pushing too hard. This could be a week, a month, or even a full season. Whatever it takes to recharge the batteries and come back with a passion for the sport.

How Parents Can Sabotage and Affect Confidence

On the flip side, there are things we can do as parents that get in the way or hold our kids back from being successful. The passage below is taken from an article published on The Compound's Rokfin channel at https://rokfin.com/CompoundStrong.

The Compound in Pennsylvania is run by Bill Bassett, the father of Bo Bassett who, at the time of writing this book, is a 15U world champion. I suspect by the time you are reading this, he's won quite a few more events.

What really piqued my interest in this article was some of the very subtle, nonverbal, and verbal things we do as parents that actually undermine the wrestlers ability to feel confident and that we trust them.

In The Compound articles, we talk a lot about the parent's part in helping their wrestler/athlete. This is because parents play the biggest role and are around their kids the most. I believe what happens between the wrestler and parents behind closed doors, plays a huge role in how your wrestler performs mentally and emotionally.

The topic we are going to get into today is having confidence in your child. I hear and see so many parents stressing and worrying about a tough wrestler that their child is about to wrestle. Some go as far as already accepting their child's defeat before they even wrestle. Your child can sense and see this. If you aren't confident, there is absolutely no way they will be. Parents and children know each other's body language better than anyone. So if you are nervous and worried, then your child is going to be really nervous and worried. Do not just verbally express your confidence, you have to physically show it. To do this, you actually have to believe it. There is no faking it—focus on the right things. You have to make your child feel like anything can be accomplished and to never put anybody on a pedestal. Don't make any match bigger than the rest. Confidence and motivation are contagious but so is not being confident.

It was easy for me to combat this situation because I am a very confident person already. I have full belief in myself and my boys/wrestlers. When my boys started wrestling, this belief and confidence instantly shifted towards them. From their very first match I believed that they were going to win. I never went into a match thinking "OMG he has a two-time state champ." At that time, they have never even been to the state tournament yet and I never believed they were going to get their butt kicked. If they did get beat badly by an individual, I have full confidence that they will win the very next time they wrestle. I also do not really know who kids are and never really got into that. That shouldn't matter, and when parents start talking and worrying about rankings and brackets, their kids will do the same. All that really matters is your child going out each match as hard as they can. If those things matter to you, then they will matter to them. Do not make it out to be a big deal if your child is wrestling a good wrestler, and especially do not let them hear you making a big deal about it. You will have them beat before they even go out onto the mat. Make it into an opportunity and challenge. This helps take pressure off of them. If your child doesn't have confidence or belief in themselves, you need to pick up their slack and really let them know that you do. Again emotions are contagious, you might think that you can hide it but you can't, especially to your family.

My advice is to always be calm, be confident, and not care who your child is about to wrestle. Only care about your child's effort and attitude. Do not focus on wins and losses. Be sure to focus on 100% effort and a good attitude then the wins will come. Believe in your children and the training they put in. Have confidence in them and ALWAYS BELIEVE IN THEM.

I thought that was a great article and has a few points that I want to expand on. The most important thing I took out of the article was how talking about other wrestlers in the bracket could make my wrestler feel not capable of winning. As a parent, talking about the seeds in a tournament or what side of the bracket you're on basically tells your wrestler that you are worried about them losing. If you are worried about them losing, you aren't confident they will win. Even if that's not what you are truly thinking, it projects even more doubt in their head than they already have.

The other takeaway I got from the article is how emotions are contagious. This makes me think also about both the verbal and non-verbal vibes we give off. By projecting our nervousness, it sends a message that we are worried about them. This could be from telling them to "watch out" for the other kid's moves, constantly asking them "are you ready?", or nervously fidgeting near them while they warm up.

In fact, there are several things I've seen that parents do over the years that can undermine a wrestler's confidence. Here are a few.

- **Putting other kids on a pedestal** – Don't say things like, "Yeah, that Johnny is a hammer. He'll probably win state this year." When elevating another wrestler over your own, it's like it's permanent and they can never be beaten. It says to your wrestler "You aren't as good as them and it's not possible to beat them." Even if your wrestler has less experience, the attitude should be, "I'm coming for you and I'm gonna close the gap each time we wrestle."

- **Comparing your kid's skills to another wrestler** – Telling someone, "You need to wrestle more like him. Watch how smooth he is," or "That kid's double leg is so explosive. You need to hit doubles like that." To your wrestler, this subconsciously sounds like "you aren't good enough."

This doesn't mean not to watch other wrestlers to emulate them, but use people they would be inspired by like an older wrestler, college, or Olympic wrestler. Plus, wrestlers have different personalities and natural skill sets. Your wrestler may not be naturally fast or explosive, so they may not be able to emulate that skill. They need to embrace who they are and build on that.

- **Profile stalking opposing wrestlers before tournaments** – Don't look up the stats and the record of their opponent before a match. Does it really matter? Will it change how they wrestle? It just makes you feel more or less nervous. If you are going to compare online profiles, you might as well not wrestle the match. Just put the two profiles side by side and whoever has the most stars on Trackwrestling wins. There's a reason you wrestle the matches.

Heck, watch any NCAA wrestling tournament. Top seeds go down all the time. No. 15-seeds make the finals. Past records do not matter. All that matters is wrestling that one match.

- **Having your wrestler scout another kid** – Please do not say "Hey, you are gonna get the winner of this match. Watch them so you can see what they do." For most kids, all this does is make them worry about that other kid. What if that kid destroys someone? Does that make them an amazing wrestler? They may have just beat a beginner. It's not like you can really prepare for someone's tendencies five minutes before your match. They should be focused on imposing their will on the other kid and being confident enough in their own abilities that it doesn't matter what the other kid will try.

This goes for scouting yourself as well and telling them "Watch out for their headlock." They'll spend the whole match worried about a headlock. If they do get headlocked, so what? Now they know what that feels like and can work on counters in practice.

- **Worrying about their ability to take on challenges** – It's common for parents to worry that if their wrestler loses or gets "beat up" that it will hurt their confidence. But this is a fear-based mindset. This way of thinking can hurt their confidence in even more detrimental ways than losing a wrestling match can. If they think that you don't believe in their ability to take on a challenge, there's no way they will believe it for themselves. Challenges are how we grow as humans and kids need to feel empowered to take them on as early as possible. They need to know their parents believe in them. Wrestling-specific examples may be:

◊ Afraid to start doing tournaments because you think they "are not ready yet"

◊ Afraid to move up from novice tournaments into the open division

◊ Afraid of other wrestlers and avoiding them in brackets

by changing weight classes because they might lose

◊ Not thinking they are "good enough" to start traveling or attending tougher events

Yelling at your kid during their match – I delve more into this later when we talk about your role during matches. But as it relates to undermining their confidence, yelling, and especially if your tone is panicked, basically tells your wrestler that you don't think they are trying hard enough to win, that you don't think they are wrestling well and that yelling instructions or "motivation" is necessary for them to win.

 How you talk to them, and about them, will shape how they see themselves, so build them up instead of tearing them down.

• **Talking about problems as if they are permanent** – Saying things like "he's just not good at takedowns" or "he has confidence issues" sound like permanent conditions that the wrestler can't overcome. Every wrestler has things they can improve on. Kids need to feel like they are making progress. That is what keeps them interested and improving in any sport, regardless if they are winning or losing. They want to feel they can master it and find success.

How you talk to them, and about them, will shape how they see themselves, so build them up instead of tearing them down. Instead, rephrase how you say things as if they are on a positive path of improving. Replace "he's just not good at takedowns" with "he's been working on his single leg and needs to keep getting reps on finishing."

Chapter 7. Parenting Wisdom For Practices and Matches

When your wrestler is in an environment where they will face challenges, your actions (and reactions) will have a significant impact. The interactions they have with their parents during these moments are critical times that will shape their experience and how they develop as a wrestler and a person. These moments allow you to help shape how they react to, and bounce back from, adversity.

This adversity not only arises from the battle of wrestling live matches at tournaments, it can also come from practice. In practice they are constantly being stretched outside of their comfort zone physically and intellectually. They will often leave beaten and exhausted. To help them grow and learn from the sport, it's important for you to understand how to handle these situations.

Sometimes it makes sense to step in and give words of advice or encouragement. Other times, even just your presence, without saying anything, can be what is best. It's important they learn how to process and deal with these emotions themselves, while still knowing you are there to support them.

Your Role At Practices

Every team is different and I don't know the age of your wrestler(s), so the following section section may not apply if you don't attend practice. Some practices are closed off to parents and others allow them to stay and watch. Most are healthy environments, but I know of some where once the live wrestling begins, the parents can start to get a little "passionate."

If you are tempted to call out to your wrestler while they are practicing or wrestling live, I know it's mostly because you want to fix their mistakes, encourage or motivate them. But you need to avoid this temptation. Because, you know what is miserable as a wrestler? Having your parents yell across the room at you during practice in front of your friends and your coach.

Would you want your boss shouting at you while you are trying to finish a project? Practices need to be an environment where they are comfortable taking risks and making mistakes. Practices are for learning and messing things up is part of that process. Your voice can be distracting and it's hard to focus. They don't need to hear your voice or look up at you while they are wrestling. In fact, several times I've seen a wrestler look at their parents for approval while wrestling and get taken down because their head was turned away.

Here are some helpful tips if you attend practices where the parents are allowed to watch:

• **Find a group of parents you can talk with** – This will help you keep your mind off analyzing your wrestler's performance. If you can't control yourself, it may be easier to stay in the car or drop off and come back at the end.

• **If you have a younger wrestler (5-8 years), either stay in the car or drop off** – Often knowing that you are there heightens their emotions. If they get knocked around, young wrestlers often look up for their mom or dad to put on a performance. "Aghhhh…look at how hurt I am." They'll cry or even run to their safe place in mom's arms. But if they don't see you, they usually just brush it off and keep wrestling.

• **Don't get frustrated if they aren't executing a move they just learned** – For most kids, the mind and body don't work that way. Learning something theoretically, when the partner isn't fighting them, is different than doing it with the pressure of a live go. They are naturally afraid to make mistakes or hit a move they aren't comfortable with yet. A few kids can immediately translate what they learned, but for most it takes trial and error, as well as time. It's important as a parent watching a practice to stay patient and let the process play out.

- **Be aware of nonverbal signals you are giving off** – I call it "Disappointed Dad Face" because it's usually the dads I've seen do this. They may not say much, but always look upset or frustrated when their wrestler isn't performing up to their expectations during practice. These nonverbal cues you give off can be just as powerful as your words. Their motivation during a practice shouldn't be to please you or prevent you from being disappointed.

- **Avoid negative criticism after practice** – Don't berate them for all the mistakes you saw them make. Again, they need to be comfortable taking risks and this will simply prevent them from doing so. If you complain about how your wrestler never takes any shots, worrying about making mistakes may be one of those reasons. Plus, you want them to enjoy the process of practice. If they associate going to practice with getting scolded in the car on the way home, they will have a negative association with it. Naturally, they won't want to go if they think this is what it means to go to practice.

If effort or attitude is an issue, this is a different subject. These should definitely be addressed if it's hindering their progress. Chatting with their friends a little between drills is one thing, but being lazy or having a bad attitude is another.

- **Encourage them to stay after** – This could be to do extra work or ask the coach a question. This builds a habit of doing extra and also lets them know it's okay to put themselves out there. This can both help build their confidence and develop a personal connection with the coach.

I have several wrestlers who, at the end of practice, say

"thank you" and shake my hand. As a coach, I appreciate this.

- **Encourage them to find tough partners** – If they are always just practicing with their friends, they may not be pushing themselves. It's okay for a parent to point this out and encourage them to find partners who are one or two levels above them. Remember, they should have three types of partners: ones they are even with, ones they can beat, and ones who can beat them.

- **Don't be afraid to talk to the coach** – Granted, don't be the annoying parent that expects the whole practice to be catered around their wrestler. But if you see your wrestler not working their hardest, it's fine to ask for a different partner or to ask the coach to address it.

Your Role on Match Day

Early on, your biggest role is simply taking them to practice and tournaments. Some parents loathe the idea of sitting in a gym all day, but this is the reality of most sports, not just wrestling.

While it may be tedious for you as a parent, getting mat time at tournaments is critical to your wrestler's development, as well as for their overall enjoyment of the sport. Just as it is the case for wrestlers, there are aspects of this sport for parents that are difficult, but they are rewarding in the end. If needed, find a group of parents you can alternate carpooling with. Friendships and relationships are a big part of enjoying the experience so traveling with friends is a smart way to do it.

Some parents are volunteer coaches and may coach from the corner, but I'm going to direct the first part of this to parents who are in the stands. I'll have a special section at the end for parents who coach.

For many parents, match days can be difficult. It's easy to get so wrapped up in wanting your wrestler to win that you lose sight of how your emotions can affect how they perform. If you are overly nervous or stressed, ask yourself why. Sports should be fun for them and you!

Here are some helpful tips for what to do, and not do, on match days.

Before matches

- **What to bring** – Concession stands are notorious for having incredibly unhealthy options for wrestlers. Having the right kind of fuel is important to perform your best. Make sure to pack water and some sort of electrolyte-fortified drinks, as well as healthy snacks, such as fruit or nutrition bars. They shouldn't have a full belly, but will need things that sustain them through a long day. I would also suggest always having athletic tape in case shoelaces come undone or they jam a finger. And for you, a comfortable seat cushion is always better than hard bleachers.

- **Brackets** – Since you are not going to worry about opposing wrestlers, there is no need to look ahead in the bracket. The only thing needed is their first match number and mat assignment. Wrestlers need to learn how to focus on one match at a time. There is no need to look and see, "If I win, I have this kid and if I lose, blah blah." They need to learn to focus on things they control, which is their own match and not other results or who they may wrestle next.

Plus, they shouldn't be worried about what happens if they lose when their goal is to win. Learning how to do this will come from modeling your behavior.

- **Warming Up** – Some coaches do a team warmup and others have the wrestlers warm up on their own. You can make sure your wrestler is ready by simply reminding them to warm up for each match. Before the tournament and their first match, they should jog, do some dynamic stretches and gymnastics, then start drilling with a partner in all positions. After that, they should "spar" or "play wrestle" at about 50% effort to simulate a match pace, without actually going live.

136

Then it's important for them to wrestle a few one- to two-minute mini-matches. Wrestlers need to get the "first-match jitters" out and get their mind into an active, high paced mode. After live wrestling, they need to make sure their lungs are opened up by doing four to five hard sprints. The lungs should burn a little. This ensures their airways are fully opened and can process oxygen more effectively. If they don't do this, they will look like they are gassing out because their airways will expand too fast and then contract, limiting oxygen flow.

If they have a long break between matches, they should repeat this sprint process or do some really hard "stance and motion" routines to open the lungs back up. This should be done about four to five matches ahead of time. If their next matches are up fairly soon, there is no need to do sprints, but they should do some dynamic stretches/bounding motions like frog jumps, or stance and motion, to get their muscles loosened up again.

• **Pre-match talk** – Honestly, there really isn't much you need to do or say to get your wrestler ready. As a parent, the inclination is to give them advice and pump them up, but really the goal should be to stay relaxed and have fun. They should be hanging out with friends or listening to music between matches. If there are any last minute tips or reminders, let the coach do that.

Parents like to ask stuff like, "Are you ready?" or "How are you feeling?" or "Make sure you are doing X, Y, Z." (i.e. remember to be in a good stance, remember, this kid has a good headlock, make sure to try that new move you just learned, etc.) Your wrestler already has a bunch of things swirling in their head and this just gets them overwhelmed with too much information.

There is no need to fill their head with more stuff. In reality, this is just your nervous energy. If you ask "Are you ready?" it's not like they are going say, "No, I'm not ready." Just project a sense of calm and confidence yourself and they will follow suit.

If you have a newer wrestler, you may get the sense that they are nervous and that's fine. Most kids are and you can remind them that the other kid is nervous too. There is no pressure, and you should make sure that you aren't adding any extra pressure they aren't already putting on themselves. Ideally, you want them to be confident, have fun, and score points. When you are free from all the pressure to compete, the scoring and winning come more naturally.

•   **Importance of a single match** – At tournaments, I've noticed that parents can make matches more important than they need to be. Unless this is the NCAA Tournament or the Olympics, matches are for practice. There is a bigger, longer-term goal than winning the county championship or Blue Eagle Open. They are just wrestling matches and there will be plenty more. Also, nobody cares about your record when you are eight years old. There's no need to get overly worked up or stressed out for "the big match with Johnny from Central."

Look, I get it. At the time there may be matches that are more important than others. And there is nothing wrong with getting fired up to compete. I think that's a good thing. My point is to have some perspective. Don't get yourself (or your wrestler) so worked up that it affects their performance in a negative way.

•   **Bribing your wrestler** – I've had some parents tell their wrestlers they will get a new game or ice cream if they win a certain match or hit a certain move. I'm not really a big fan of this. Yeah, it may temporarily spark extra motivation, but they will be motivated for the wrong reasons.

What happens when the next match comes around? Do they get more ice cream or money then? Do they keep getting it the rest of their career? I don't mind if it's done in a playful way or some little fun side bet for executing a move, but I'd rather their motivation come from within and not a reward. The win or loss should fuel their training at practice. The desire to win or hatred of losing should be what motivates them for the long haul, not an external short-term bribe.

During matches

Again, this assumes you are watching from the stands or near the mat, not coaching. If you end up having to jump in their corner, I have some tips for you in just a little bit.

Simply put, once the match starts, as a parent there is nothing you can do. This is their wrestling match that they have trained for. Let them wrestle and enjoy that you have the opportunity to watch them compete. I know the emotions you are going through. The best advice I can give you is don't be *that* parent who is screaming at their kid throughout the match.

Cheering them on is one thing, but when you are yelling, they can't hear the coach. They need to be trained to listen to their coach's voice. And I know you think they will wrestle better if you just yell just over the crowd or repeat what the coach says but just a little louder. But in reality, they are pausing just a little every time you yell. Or worse, looking at you during their match. You have been an authority figure in their life and they don't want to disappoint you. So every time they hear you, they are not focused on wrestling through the next position. Or they are afraid to take a risk because they don't want to make a mistake and disappoint you.

They need to build confidence in their abilities and that comes from being in the moment—not being distracted or relying on motivation from their parents. And especially if they are new or young...think about their association with the sport. If they associate wrestling with their dad or mom seeming mad or yelling throughout the match, why would they want to continue?

Even if you think you are just shouting "encouragements" or telling them moves they should hit, *they* can easily think you are yelling and disappointed. Also, if this is you, record yourself sometime. If they are losing, how much panic or disappointment is in your tone? What if there are 30 seconds left? "You gotta go! Shoot! What are you doing?!" If you are panicked, they are panicked. It's hard to learn to stay calm under pressure when everyone around you is freaking out.

I had a wrestler a few years ago whose dad wanted to be on the mat beside me when I coached. All he did was yell the same things I was saying, but by that time, the moment for that move had passed. His son would freeze every time his dad yelled, and the dad's reaction was that he "needed to suck it up." But that's not what sucking it up means.

Why would you create more stress for your wrestler when they are fighting their hardest already? Eventually the dad understood that his antics were making his son wrestle worse and I told him he wasn't allowed on the mat anymore. He had to watch from the stands. Almost immediately his son started wrestling better and went from a losing wrestler to a multiple-time youth state placer and finalist.

The best thing you can do while they are wrestling is record their matches. This will force you to stay calm, but also give them and their coach an opportunity to watch the match back to learn.

After matches

The conclusion of a match can be a critical time that determines how a wrestler will develop both in their skills and confidence. Remember that someone has to win and someone has to lose. Losing is just part of the sport and part of your role is to help them understand how to deal with the adversity of losing in a healthy way. How you respond is just as important as how they respond. I've seen parents yell at their kid after a match, then threaten to take them home because they didn't get a pin for their dual team. This type of behavior from a parent is unacceptable. Help them learn how to evaluate matches without emotion by writing down notes after each match. They should quickly document what they did well and what they need to work on. This process goes a long way to both speeding up the learning process, but also incorporating this evaluation skill into their life.

- **After wins** – Compliment the skills and effort, not

just the result. Ask what they did that caused them to do well. This way they understand why and will associate that behavior with success. You are trying to reinforce the behavior that led to the win, not the win itself. Examples could be "Wow, great comeback. You had to dig deep for that one." or "That was a beautiful takedown. Is that something you've been working on in practice?"

• **After losses** – Some kids take losses harder than others. If they are emotional, give them a few minutes before talking to them (and you may need a few minutes yourself). I cannot stress this enough. Nobody likes to lose. And hating to lose can actually be a major driver for success. Unless they are throwing a major tantrum, there is no need to talk to them until they've calmed down.

As a coach, I almost always give some advice after a match, but if they are upset I tell them to cool off for a bit and then come back to see me. How should you, as the parent, talk to them after a loss? Remember your role is as mom or dad, not coach. Let the coach address technical areas they can improve on. But you can be there to help them through the mental and emotional part of dealing with adversity. Here are a few tips:

◊ **Recognize the positive** – Even if they lose, they need to learn how to identify some of the good things they did out there. This may simply be acknowledging effort and not giving up, but also could be a skill they executed.

◊ **Losses are for learning** – Let them know that losses are actually a good thing despite how much that feeling sucks. It's just part of the process. Ask them what they can work on from that match and also what they did well. Again, it's about the process not the result, so they need to know if they have made progress in their skills regardless of the loss. A good coach will give them something tangible to learn from that they can apply to the next match or they can make a note of something they need to work on at practice.

Losing doesn't mean you are bad at wrestling. The best wrestlers in the world still lose. In fact, if they aren't losing they aren't challenging themselves enough to get better. I used to have something written on the wall in practice that said:

How do you deal with losing?

A: Make excuses (the ref screwed me, etc.)

B. Pity party (poor me, I must suck at wrestling)

C. Take accountability (ask "What can I learn?" and "What action will I take to improve?")

You alway have a choice. Turn the failure into an action.

◊ **Short memory** – If they are in a tournament, help them learn to deal with their emotions and then move on. The next match will be up soon and they need to be ready. They are allowed to have a couple minutes to calm down and then they can refocus their energy on improving for the next one.

You can't take emotional baggage with you into the next match. Each match is a new opportunity. Part of your (and the coach's) role is to teach them how to not dwell in the past. You can't go back in a time machine to wrestle the match again or play the "woulda, coulda, shoulda" game. That match is over now and you can't control it. The only thing to do is move forward.

 As a parent, you want your wrestler to take full accountability after their loss. In turn, you must also model that behavior.

◊ **Outbursts should not be tolerated** – Getting upset is understandable. Crying, believe it or not, is fine too. They aren't weak if they cry when they are young. This means they cared enough to win and often they are just physically and emotionally exhausted. However, if they throw their headgear or make a scene on the mat, they need to apologize to both their coach and the opponent's coach. If their behavior is really bad, feel free to take them home. Obviously, this is a judgment call, but they need

142

to know what is acceptable and unacceptable behavior.

◊ **Don't make excuses** – As a parent, you want your wrestler to take full accountability for their loss. This helps them take ownership over what to improve on. In turn, you must also model that behavior.

As a fun topic in a group chat with other wrestling dads we started a list of excuses that kids often make for losing. We then quickly realized it was actually excuses that the parents make. Not just after matches, but often before matches as a way to say "Well, in case they lose or look bad, here are all the reasons why." What began as a short list morphed into 38.

Some of these are for fun, but most are real excuses we've heard over the years. Maybe you've said some of these before?

Parent's list of excuses for losing

1. They were feeling sick
2. Just felt "off" today
3. Didn't cut enough weight/too small for the weight class
4. The ref robbed us/bad call
5. Need to get cardio up/out of shape
6. Haven't wrestled in a while/still knocking off the rust
7. Got a bad draw in the bracket
8. Got "caught" in a move
9. Didn't care about winning. Just gathering intel for later.
10. Got too emotional
11. Had a bad weight cut/felt drained
12. Didn't recover right from the weight cut (ate the wrong things, didn't drink enough)
13. That kid was "jacked"
14. We're not serious right now and haven't been training hard
15. Was just trying new moves
16. Not "feeling good" mentally/wasn't in the zone
17. Didn't get enough sleep
18. We're hurt/dinged up right now

143

19. Coach screwed us (picked the wrong position, yelled the wrong move)
20. Senioritis
21. Big match pressure just got to us
22. Thinking too much
23. The other kid is in his head (never can beat this kid)
24. It's just a bad style matchup for us
25. The other kid got lucky
26. Didn't get a good warm up
27. The other kid had a tattoo
28. Haven't adjusted to new weight class yet
29. Kid has a famous coach
30. Ate/drank too much right before my match
31. The other kid stalled the whole match
32. We pinned ourselves
33. "Satellite weigh-ins" (there's no way that other kid was the same weight class)
34. We're at the bottom of the age group
35. Didn't have a coach in the corner
36. It was the first match of the day/first-match jitters
37. Loses in consolation bracket match (I already beat him on front side, so it didn't matter)
38. The other dude has a beard

Tips for Parents Who Also Coach

This was me. I coached my son from when he was four years old until he graduated high school. I know how tricky it is navigating this complex social dynamic. I'm not saying I was perfect and every kid is different, but here is my advice to you:

• **Separate your roles** – Be the coach at practice, but when you get in the car or at home, you are the parent. It's very tempting to want to call out the mistakes they made at practice or constantly give them ways to improve their wrestling. It's not a bad thing to talk about wrestling at home or anything, but don't always make it about them. Enjoy that you have a special bond together and don't feel like you always have to give them coaching advice.

• **Find other coaches to help them** – As much as you want to mold them and have direct control over their development, it's much better when you have someone you trust to work with them. I do think you can successfully get away with being their primary coach until they are about eight to 10, but after that they will be way more receptive to someone they view as their coach.

• **Help them feel like they are making progress** – This goes for all wrestlers you coach, but it's easy to be more critical of your son or daughter. Everyone has things to improve on, but you are with them everyday so you see all the little things. They can end up perceiving that you think they are never good enough.

In your conversations about their wrestling, make them feel they are on an upward trajectory, even if there are tons of things they need to work on. Pick and choose the high-impact things to focus on and as mentioned several times in this book, help them take ownership over those. Collaborate with them on their action plan versus always telling them what they need to work on.

• **Stay patient** – You see all the potential in them and it's easy to want to rush the process with your own child. The most important thing is that they are motivated and they see progress. Treat them like any other wrestler you have in terms of how much and when to push them to higher levels.

• **It's not about you** – You are a coach so in the back of your mind you feel like their wrestling is a reflection of you. So losses sting a little more and you have a little more panic when matches are close. You may even feel embarrassed if they wrestle badly. But their winning or losing isn't a reflection of you and your coaching abilities unless you make it that way. Each kid's path is unique, including your own.

Remember, David was 13-76 his first five years of wrestling but I stayed patient and encouraged him to stick with it. I pointed out when he was making progress and tried to help him find ways to keep improving.

• **In the practice room** – I found that many parents who coach tend to hover near their kid during practice. I tell anyone who has ever helped me out that the only rule I have is to not coach your own kid. Try to have another coach work that side of the room so they aren't so worried about you. They will focus better and get more out of practice.

Plus, when you get so focused on your own child, it's easy to take attention away from the other wrestlers in the room. It also decreases your own stress level if you're not worried about whether they are doing the moves right.

• **During matches** – If you have another coach who can help, have them be in the corner so you can back away from the mat. I know you want to have a more hands-on role and you know your wrestler better than anyone else, but trust me, it's better in the long run.

If you don't have that ability and have to be in the corner, remember that your wrestler will have a hard time seeing you in both roles. You have to remember that what they hear is not just your words (and most of the time they can't hear you through the head gear, crowd and whistles anyway). But they hear your tone and they pick up on your nonverbal cues.

Are you really helping them through a match or are you upset that they didn't finish a takedown or are laying on their belly on bottom? As difficult as it might be to separate yourself from it, try to observe how your words and tone are affecting how they are wrestling (in a good or bad way).

If you do end up being in their corner, here are some simple tips you can follow to improve your coaching skills:

◊ **Let them wrestle through a position** – You don't always have to tell them what to do. This will help their brain make the connection and build their confidence when they do the right thing.

◊ **Keep notes** – They should be the one taking notes but if they are younger, it can help if you jot down any trends or specific issues they can work on.

◊ **Know the rules** – There is nothing worse than yelling "That's two!" and it's not actually a takedown. Or even worse, getting in a fight with the ref because they missed a call and they don't overturn it. The appendix of this book includes some basics about rules and scoring, as well as pictures of positions where the rules are commonly misapplied. It also includes tips for how to approach referees during matches.

◊ **Hold your advice** – Follow my same advice that I gave earlier. Don't feel like you have to give them advice right away. If they win, give them a high five and compliment something they did well. If they lose, give them some time to cool off and ask them ways they feel like they can improve. Help them own it and take accountability for the loss so they can keep working on their skills in practice.

What to say and not to say during matches

• **Be specific** – i.e. "Shift your right hand to the elbow or slide your left knee under"

• **Avoid big adult words** – Use simple words they will understand.

• **Tell them what to do, rather than what NOT to do** – This gives them a specific action to execute (examples: "Keep your head up" versus "Stop putting your head down" or "Snap his head before shooting" vs. "Stop diving for your shots"). If you say stop diving for your shots, they may just not shoot at all.

• **Focus on the present, not the past** – Don't critique a

situation during a match that already happened. That position is over with. Take a note and work on that in practice

- **Don't yell and get their attention just to say nothing of value** – "Hey...hey...hey! Look at me....Let's go!" (Wait, you spent all that time to get their attention as if you had some magic secret move you wanted them to remember to hit and all you wanted to do is say "let's go"?

- **Avoid these common (and completely ineffective) phrases**

◊   *"Don't do anything stupid"* – Thanks dad, I'll try not to.

◊   *"Watch out for the ....."* – When they are focused on the other wrestler, they aren't executing their own moves.

◊   *"What are you doing?!!!"* – Do you really think they are going to answer you? I've seen kids turn back to their parents and say "I'm trying" and then get scored on.

◊   *"Be smart"* – What does that actually mean? What exactly are you asking them to do?

◊   *"Just get up!"* – Thanks Dad, it's that easy.

◊   *"Shoot! Just shoot!!!"* – Then they shoot..."Damnit, why are you diving at their legs!" (well, uh, Dad, you told me to just shoot even though the shot wasn't there to take.)

CONCLUSION

I hope this book helped you gain perspective on not only what it takes to succeed in the sport of wrestling, but also how to support your wrestler along their journey. As a parent, you are a major influence over their development as a person and if wrestling becomes a big part of their life, then it will be part of yours.

This book talks about how learning to succeed in wrestling isn't just about the wins, but also about the life lessons it teaches. Your job is to help them apply those lessons to the rest of their life experiences. Just a few of these lessons are:

- Bouncing back from adversity
- The process of success and embracing failure as a learning tool
- Sacrificing in the short term for a long-term goal
- Embracing your strengths and weaknesses, while learning how to continuously improve
- Taking accountability
- Not giving up when things get hard
- Dealing with self-doubt, fear, and other psychological factors
- Performing under pressure
- Being grateful

So what actions can you take now?

1.   Ask them what their goals are. What do they want to get out of wrestling? Why do they like the sport? Everything will stem from their internal motivations. While they may not even know the answers yet, as a parent you should seek to understand what makes them tick.

2.   Define three to five of your own personal takeaways from the book and actions you plan to take as a result

3.   If you'd like to get more information such as the weight management guide, college recruiting guide, or articles about common skin infections, injuries, or other topics, visit parents. levelupwrestling.com. You can subscribe to be notified when new content is posted.

4.   If you like what I had to say, follow me on social media. I try to post more valuable content for both parents, wrestlers and coaches. My Twitter handle is @donovanpanone and my Instagram is @levelupwrestling.

One of the most important takeaways that I hope you found in this book is that they have to want it for themselves. As they get older, the control and influence you have will slowly lessen. You have to trust that you've done the right things early on for them to develop a love for the sport and to embrace the process of success.

But ultimately it's on them. You can support them and try to place them in positive situations. Surround them with good people and love them no matter what. Hold them accountable to the goals they set but remember to keep it fun.

Remember that every child has unique strengths and weaknesses and will go through their own journey. If you do everything right, they might go on to find high-level success in wrestling...but they may not. And that's okay. They will find the path that they are meant for. The foundation you help them build through the sport of wrestling will enable them to find success in anything they do.

Appendix
UNDERSTANDING THE
RULES OF WRESTLING

This section isn't just for parents who are new to wrestling. It's also for anyone who doesn't understand why referees make certain calls or will help clarify common situations where an incorrect call is made. This will help make watching a match a lot easier to understand. Keep in mind that these will be based on the Folkstyle NFHS 2022 Rulebook and could change over time.

Basic Difference between Folkstyle, Freestyle, and Greco-Roman

There are several forms of wrestling and grappling around the world. In the U.S., we primarily focus on folkstyle, freestyle and Greco-Roman wrestling. Folkstyle is the most popular and is performed in high school, college, and is the primary youth style during the winter sports season from about November to February and March, depending on where you live.

In the spring, for many the focus shifts to the Olympic styles of wrestling. These are freestyle and Greco-Roman (a.k.a. "Greco") which are the most popular worldwide. During the summer, there are national freestyle and Greco events that occur but some opt to attend folkstyle events. This is mostly personal preference or what your school or club focuses on. Like most sports, wrestling can be year-round if you choose.

The primary difference between freestyle, Greco-Roman, and folkstyle is what happens after the takedown. In freestyle and Greco, the bottom person does not try to escape. The top wrestler has about 15 seconds to turn their opponents back past 90 degrees. If unsuccessful, they return back to the standing position again. The other major difference is that in freestyle and Greco, at any time a wrestler's action causes the other wrestler's back to go past 90 degrees, they will earn points regardless if a takedown has occurred. Folkstyle and freestyle are very similar on the feet with the same basic takedowns. But in Greco-Roman you cannot use or touch the legs. The best way to understand the differences is to watch a few YouTube videos and you will see for yourself. It's all wrestling, though, and important to learn all three styles. Many of the Olympic-style skills translate into folkstyle success.

Folkstyle Rules Simplified

While this is an appendix not a comprehensive rulebook, parents often get confused as to why a certain position is scored a certain way. Since folkstyle is the primary style, we'll focus on that here.

Takedowns

The rulebook defines a takedown as "when, from the neutral position (standing), a wrestler gains control over the opponent down on the mat and a total of two supporting points of either wrestler are inbounds." So then you are probably asking "what do they mean by control?" Instead of using words, the rulebook uses pictures. Basically, once you get them to the mat you either need to be behind their arms and hips or put them on their back. A takedown is worth two points. Here are a few pictures of a basic takedown and when it occurs.

This is a pretty typical position where a takedown has occurred (see Example 1).

Some takedowns are clear and obvious, but some wrestling positions can be questionable whether someone has "control" or not. Here are some of the more questionable positions that referees often get wrong.

Examples 2 and 3 get called incorrectly all the time. I'm notorious for coming up to the table with my rulebook picture explaining why they missed the call. I'm usually polite about it, but I also know they don't like a smug coach challenging their ego. I'm really not. I just like accuracy and the rulebook is pretty clear. Inexperienced refs (or even refs who have done it a long time, but aren't using the actual rulebook) will often say, "Coach, he still had your wrestler's leg, that's not control." Or "Coach, he has to cover the hip completely for it to be a takedown."

You can see that the rulebook clearly says it's a takedown even though the opponent's arms are still

Example 1
A takedown is scored when the defensive wrestler's legs are controlled above or below the knees and the majority of the wrestler's weight is supported by the hands.

Example 2
There is control by the wrestler on top if this position is held beyond reaction time, even though the hands of the opponent are locked around a leg.

Example 3
There is control by the wrestler on top even though the hands of the opponent are locked around a leg. The top wrestler has the opponent off the base and is hip to hip.

153

Example 4
This is a takedown regardless of the body lock by the wrestler in the dark uniform.

Example 5
The crotch lift does not stop the takedown by the wrestler in the light uniform.

around the leg. The main difference between these two positions is reaction time. In the first one, the opponent is still on his knees. If this position was only for a split second and then adjusted, it wouldn't be beyond a reaction time and thus be a takedown. In the second picture, the opponent is flat on their belly. This position doesn't require the reaction time.

Examples 4 and 5, where the opponent is sitting on their butt and the offensive wrestler is locked around their legs, can also be miscalled often, but are also kinda tricky. Refs often wait until the offensive wrestler builds up around the waist to call a takedown. This is incorrect and just something that has been a misconception over time. But in these pictures, the offensive wrestler is parallel and covering the opponent's legs with their

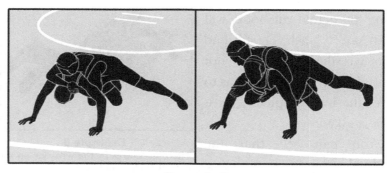

Example 6
In these two situations with the leg trapped, there is control by the wrestler on top. This is a takedown.

154

body. If the opponent's legs were off to one side and legs were curled back a bit, this would not be considered control yet.

This takedown position in Example 6 is also often called incorrectly. Personally, I don't think it should be a takedown, but it is. It's also a position known as a "merkle." A merkle is defined when they are both side by side, with one wrestler's leg snaking inside the other and applying a side headlock, basically locking up the head and arm together. The key to saying this is control is that the wrestler's toes are snaked around and hooking the calf. For some reason, a picture of the traditional merkle with the head and arm locked is not actually in the rulebook. But the two positions in the pictures are not often called as takedowns.

I actually won a call for my wrestler in a big overtime match one time with my knowledge of this position. The ref was adamant that you had to have a side headlock for control. I showed him this picture and he was like "Well, damn. I learned something today."

Escapes

A basic escape is pretty simple. The wrestler starts in the bottom position or has been taken down. They get to their feet, face the opponent and create separation. This is worth one point. The key points here are that they face their opponent and create separation. If they simply run away with their back to them and the opponent catches up to get behind them again or attack their legs, this is not an escape. Or if they do face them on the feet and the top wrestler keeps them tied up underneath in a front headlock (locking their arm and head together), this is not an escape.

In some cases, a big scramble can ensue and a "loss of control" may occur. It's hard to explain in words, but this usually happens either going out of bounds or at the end of a period where the top wrestler is no longer in control beyond a reaction time but the bottom wrestler hasn't fully escaped.

Reversals

Reversals, worth two points, are pretty cut and dry. The person on bottom improves their position by immediately getting on top. All the positions in the rulebook that constitute a takedown and control apply to a reversal except one; a standing reversal.

The rulebook states, "It is a reversal when the defensive wrestler comes from underneath and gains control of the opponent, either on the mat or in a rear-standing position, while the total of two supporting points are inside or on the boundary line." So basically, if a wrestler starts on bottom and starts to get behind the other wrestler but they stand up, if they successfully get behind them, it's still a reversal even if both wrestlers are standing.

Near-fall/Back points

The official definition is, "Criteria for a near-fall occurs when any part of both shoulders or both scapulae of the defensive wrestler are held within 4 inches of the mat or less; or when one shoulder or scapula of the defensive wrestler is touching the mat and the other shoulder or scapula is held at an angle of 45 degrees or less with the mat; or when the defensive wrestler is held in a high bridge or on both elbows."

I get so infuriated when refs start calling back points when the back breaks 90 degrees (the back is straight up and perpendicular to the mat). I rarely ever get this call overturned. During the times that I have, I've just politely asked "What did you see?" If they say "I saw the back break 90 degrees," then I know I can make a case and explain that the rulebook says 45 degrees. What often gets missed (by myself included) is that while the angle may appear to be more than 45 degrees, the bottom of the scapula can push out causing the angle to be closer to the mat.

The rule of the back being less than 4 inches above the mat or in a high bridge can mess some coaches up. Technically, a high bridge could make someone be more than 4 inches above the mat, but it's still considered back points.

Pins (also known as falls)

The rulebook definition of a fall (or pin) is, "A fall occurs when any part of both shoulders or both scapula of either wrestler are in contact with the mat for two seconds. The two seconds (one-thousand-one, one-thousand-two) shall be a

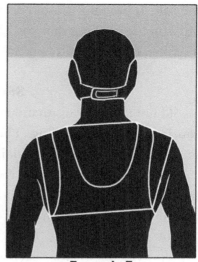

Example 7
This rear view shows a wrestler's pinning area.

silent count and shall start only after the referee is in position to observe if a fall is imminent. A fall is imminent when any part of both shoulders or both scapula of either wrestler are in contact with the mat. The shoulders or scapula must be held in continuous contact with the mat. A fall terminates wrestling."

Where parents and wrestlers get confused and often go crazy is when the bottom of the pinning area (the lower part of the scapula) are on the mat but the top of the shoulders appear to be off the mat. Or often it's that one shoulder is off the mat, but the scapula isn't. So it really looks like they aren't pinned. But that whole area, from the bottom of the scapula to the tops of the shoulders and trapezius, is part of the pinning criteria.

The part of the rule that is the most inconsistently called, however, is how long you have to hold someone down. The rulebook clearly says two seconds. But some refs will call it immediately, while some refs seem to wait forever. And obviously the parents and the coaches don't know this rule so everyone seems to be going nuts. I would say that most refs will wait about a second and most coaches have been conditioned to think this is the rule. It probably should be changed this way. In either case, a pin is not something that you can challenge the call on. So once it's done, it's done.

Stalling

There are several situations in the rulebook that define what can be considered stalling. The first stall call is a warning, the second and third result in a point for the other wrestler, a fourth call is two points, and a fifth results in a disqualification. Rather than go through each specific definition in the rulebook, I'll provide a quick summary so you can understand it better as a parent.

The rulebook says "each wrestler is required to make an honest attempt to stay within the 10-foot circle and wrestle aggressively, regardless of position or the time or score of the match." When you are avoiding this, it's considered stalling. Stalling usually happens when a wrestler is winning and trying to hold on to the lead, on the edge of the mat and trying to avoid a takedown or on bottom and trying to avoid being turned. Here's usually how the ref will make these calls.

- **Backing off the mat** – When you turn your back to the opponent and run off the mat, or backpedal off the mat without any attempt to circle back in, usually to avoid a takedown.
- **Pushing off the mat** – Often in the top position when the other wrestler is attempting an escape, the top wrestler runs them out of bounds.
- **Riding the hips on top** – If the top wrestler stays parallel and never makes an attempt to turn the bottom wrestler. Even if the bottom wrestler is not trying to come up, usually the top wrestler will be warned for stalling first.
- **Balling up on bottom** – If the bottom wrestler stays on their belly or pulls their arms tight to their side and makes no attempt to get up, they will usually be warned for stalling.

How to approach referees and *hopefully* get more calls

While I recommend that someone else coach your wrestler, sometimes you don't have a choice. So if you are in the corner and you think a call was incorrect, here are some tips to increase your chances of getting the call overturned.

Believe it or not, there is an art to talking to referees. Despite what you might think, they are human just like you and should be treated as such. Not only should you be a good role model for your wrestler, there is also a shortage of referees and being yelled at by parents and coaches doesn't help. Many have been conditioned by abusive coaches and can also be on guard before a tournament even starts, expecting to have to hold their ground. Many are even taught to not give in to coaches so that it sets a tone for a smoother tournament and they aren't constantly being challenged. This article will help you break down that guard so you can have a friendly, human-to-human conversation.

This section also has contributions from Nolan Meadors II, one of the top officials in the nation. Nolan has an M1 status for USA Wrestling and UWW3 for International events for freestyle and Greco. He has officiated at the US Open and Fargo, among several other national events. His notes have been designated with NM.

Also, these tips are about getting accurate calls based on the rulebook, not manipulating them into getting your way. Make sure you thoroughly read the rulebook so you know what you are talking about, otherwise you will look like an idiot. It used to be available on Amazon as a paperback or Kindle version, but recently they have created their own NFHS Rulebook App. This can be downloaded and is very inexpensive. Well worth it.

N.M. – First thing is to know your rulebook, not just to know wrestling, but to know the rules. Your understanding of the rulebook shouldn't be able to stick it to the refs whenever they miss a call, but to coach your kids in the best positions to win those calls. This will better allow for you to make **proper** decisions on what calls you need to argue.

Tips for Communicating with Referees

• **Become friendly with them before and after the tournament** – They are much more willing to talk with someone they like versus a coach they think is a jerk.

• **Do not question their judgment** – There are certain calls that you will not agree with and you will naturally see things in a biased lens for your wrestler. If you question their judgment they will give you a warning for Coach's Misconduct so make sure you are asking about the misapplication of a rule. Some common examples of judgment calls include:

◊ *Stalling* – Make sure you know exactly what the ref is looking for and what the rules are. Either way, it's often their judgment and likely not going to be overturned.

◊ *Loss of control* – An escape is pretty clear cut, but it's often up to the ref's judgment if the top wrestler has lost control in a flurry.

◊ *Out of bounds* – While there are specific rules for being out of bounds, it's hard to question what the ref saw.

◊ *Illegal moves* – If they didn't see it, then unfortunately they can't rule against it

• **Do not get emotional** – If you yell something from the corner like "That was BS! That's not a takedown!", there is no way you are getting that call overturned. You just put their defenses up and no matter what you say (even if you are right), they will not budge.

• **Pick your spots** – Sometimes it might be a gray area between a judgment call and a rule misapplication and you are not sure if you should approach the table. Is your kid dominating the match or getting destroyed? Might be best to let this one be.

Tournaments are long and you don't want referees already on guard because you are nitpicking every situation. Plus, if you approach the table about a rule misapplication and you are wrong, they can technically give you a yellow card for Coach's Misconduct. Most referees will not do that, but some will. Be sure that you are correct.

• **Do not yell from the corner** – I know it's hard not to do this. I'm guilty of it at times. If you have a question about a call, that's what the table is for. Some refs will not make the call simply because you were trying to manipulate it from the corner. Are there some where you can say "that's two," "stalling," or "there's the pin," and it plants a seed in their mind to make the call? Sure. They are usually younger and more inexperienced. You need to know who you are dealing with first. And really, it's usually best to just let the refs make the call and if it was inaccurate, approach the table.

• **Have an exact picture or rule ready to go** – Download the NFHS app on your phone so you always have it. The NFHS app is free and the rulebook is cheap. I also suggest getting the case book that goes over situations and common interpretations of the rules.

N.M. – Never try to use moves to constitute control or loss of control. If you read the rule book, there is no move that is solely listed as "control." (i.e. Having a cradle locked up isn't always a takedown). The ones that are have pictures elaborating on the **position** of why it is control. Your better understanding and ability to elaborate the positions/change of directions that occur in the match will better allow for you to get calls changed in your favor.

How to properly approach the table
This can make or break your ability to get an accurate call. Don't storm up there with an attitude. Calmly get the attention of

the referee (i.e. raising your hand and walking toward the table) and ask a question. Simply say something like "I have a question about a rule," "I just have a question about that situation," or "I just have a question about what you saw."

> N.M. – Approach the table as calmly as you know how (as calmly as you would want someone to approach you). This creates less initial confrontation and makes it easier for you to be heard as you ask your questions.
>
> Good rule of thumb, never tell a referee "what happened" or "what your kid did" in order to clarify a different score. First thing out of your mouth needs to be, "What did you see?"
>
> Since the referee can only call what he sees, getting an understanding from their vantage point will help. After that, if you feel inclined you may ask if they did see something else. Do not ask, "Is it possible?" Whatever the scenario is, it is always possible, but that doesn't mean that it happened.

Below are a few ways to ask a question that can lead to better results:

*   **"What did you see?"** – As Meadors states, this is massively important. Before challenging a rule make sure the ref saw the same thing you did. Otherwise everything you are questioning is irrelevant, or if they saw it differently it may not actually be a misapplication of the rule. As mentioned above, you can get called for Coach's Misconduct if you are wrong about a rule misapplication. So by asking "What did you see?" you are not saying they are wrong yet.
    ◊ *You:* "Hey John, just curious what you saw in that situation"
    ◊ *Ref:* "I saw your wrestler attempt to go behind the other wrestler, but the other wrestler still had his leg."
    ◊ *You:* "Did you see that my wrestler hooked the opponent's leg with his leg beyond reaction time?"
    ◊ *Ref:* "Yeah, but the other guy still had his arm locked

162

around his leg and your wrestler never fully covered his hip."

◊ *You:* "Okay. The rulebook actually doesn't require the hip to be covered. It shows an exact picture of what just happened and says, 'There is control by the wrestler on top if this position is held beyond reaction time, even though the hands of the opponent are locked around a leg.' Here's a picture of it."

◊ *Ref:* "Well dang, you are right. Two points for the takedown."

• **Clarify exactly what you are asking** – If it's vague, you and the official might not be talking about the same thing. Use very specific language or you can ask "Was it A or B?" Now that they have clarified "B" you can then ask. "Okay, so if it was B, then the rule states 'XYZ', correct?"

• **What does the rulebook say about that position or situation?** – If you already know the answer here, the goal isn't to play "gotcha" with the ref. He'll feel offended and think you are a smart ass. The goal is to discuss the position and gain clarity on how he's interpreting it. By talking through it, they may come to the conclusion that they made a mistake on their own. If they do this, they won't feel you are manipulating them and become stubborn.

N.M. – Do not use your resume as an argument. "I've been doing this for x amount of years and I've never heard of that call." This is one of the best examples to show that you have not read your rulebook. Someone like me who has only been officiating for eight years can come back with the numerous national championship tournaments, national awards, and recognition as an official, as well as my UWW classification to show I'm more involved in the sport than whatever coach decides to pull that card.

Hopefully this helps. Be friendly, know the rules, don't question their judgment and be specific when you ask a question about a rule. If you follow these tips, your tournaments will be less stressful and you'll get more calls go your way....assuming you were right!

ACKNOWLEDGMENTS

My wife, Jenni – For being an incredible person, my moral compass and supporting me in following my passion to coach wrestling as a career. Thank you for putting up with all those years of late practices and tournaments that never seemed to finish on time.

David – For believing in yourself and never giving up on the sport. You are a model for others to follow and have inspired more wrestlers and parents than you realize.

Kate and Cameron – Wrestling trips and nightly practices meant time away from you guys. Thank you for the sacrifices you had to make in order for me to have a career coaching wrestling.

Jeff Hilimire – For inspiring me to write and helping me define my purpose.

Blaine Hess – For being my coaching partner for 21 years and not killing me when I opened Level Up.

Arturo Holmes – For encouraging me to open my own training center despite the fact that we would be competitors. You are truly selfless.

Coach P. – For grabbing me in the hallway at school, telling me that I didn't have a choice to wrestle. You sparked a fire in me that has lasted over 32 years.

My mom & dad – In addition to being amazing parents, if it wasn't for saving my high school wrestling team after they cut the program, who knows where I would be.

My family of Pope Jr. wrestling parents and wrestlers – Not only did you help me grow as a coach, you helped my son stick with a sport he loves.

And finally, to all the "crazy wrestling parents" who gave me great stories for the book!

ABOUT THE AUTHOR

Donovan Panone didn't begin wrestling until high school and wasn't the most accomplished wrestler. After a brief stint in college wrestling, he immediately began volunteering as a coach in 1994. Since then, he has dedicated his life to decoding the formula for developing successful wrestlers. Even as a volunteer, he would obsess over technique and the best methods of teaching. He continued to find ways to improve his coaching and leadership skills.

Once he opened Level Up wrestling and began coaching full-time in 2015, he's been able to see the fruits of his labor and has produced numerous state and national champions, including Super 32 champs, Fargo champs, and winners of Flowrestling's Who's #1. He has shown that you don't need personal wrestling accolades to be a successful coach.

After years of dispensing advice, he realized there was nothing documented to help parents navigate the world of wrestling. He felt a calling to share his knowledge and experiences in hopes of having a positive effect on the lives of wrestling families. Hence this book was born.

Donovan and his wife, Jenni, live in Marietta, Georgia, and are the parents of three children. You can find more info about Level Up Wrestling Center, as well as additional resources for wrestling parents and coaches, at www.levelupwrestling.com.